5-Minute Spanish

Berlitz Publishing

New York   Munich   Singapore

5–MINUTE SPANISH

Contacting the Editors
Every effort has been made to provide accurate information in this publication, but changes are inevitable. The publisher cannot be responsible for any resulting loss, inconvenience or injury. We would appreciate it if readers would call our attention to any errors or outdated information by contacting Berlitz Publishing, 193 Morris Avenue, Springfield, NJ 07081, USA. E-mail: comments@berlitzbooks.com

First Printing: July 2009
Printed in Singapore
ISBN 978-981-268-456-1

Publishing Director: Sheryl Olinsky Borg
Senior Editor/Project Manager: Lorraine Sova, Nela Navarro
Cover Design: Claudia Petrilli
Interior Design, Composition and Editorial: Booklinks Publishing Services
Production Manager: Elizabeth Gaynor
Cover: © Marish/Dreamstime.com

Contents

Contents

How to Use This Book

By using *5-Minute Spanish* every day, you can start speaking Spanish in just minutes. The 5-Minute program introduces you to a new language and gets you speaking right away. Take a few minutes before or after work, before you go to sleep at night or any time that feels right to work on one lesson a day. If you want, you can even go ahead and do two lessons a day. Just have fun while you learn; you'll be speaking Spanish in no time.

- The book is divided into 99 lessons. Each provides a bite-sized learning opportunity that you can complete in minutes.

- Each unit has 8 lessons presenting important vocabulary, phrases and other information needed in everyday Spanish.

- A review at the end of each unit provides an opportunity to test your knowledge before you move on.

- Unless otherwise noted, *5-Minute Spanish* uses formal language. In everyday Spanish, the formal is usually used between adults who are not close friends or family and in professional settings. The informal is used with familiar friends and family and when addressing children.

¡Buenos días!

- Real life language and activities introduce the vocabulary, phrases and grammar covered in the lessons that follow. You'll see dialogues, postcards, e-mails and other everyday correspondence in Spanish.

- You can listen to the dialogues, articles, e-mails and other presentations on the *5-Minute Spanish* audio CD.

Smart Phrases

- In these lessons you'll find useful everyday phrases. You can listen to these phrases on the audio program.

- Extra Phrases enrich your knowledge and understanding of everyday Spanish. These are not practiced in the activities, but they're there for those who want to learn more.

Words to Know

- Core Words are important words related to the lesson topic. In some lessons these words are divided into sub-categories. You can listen to these words on our audio program.

- Extra Words are other helpful words to know.

Smart Grammar

- Don't let the name scare you. Smart Grammar covers the basic parts of speech you'll need to know if you want to speak Spanish easily and fluently.

- From verb usage to forming questions, the 5-Minute program provides quick and easy explanations and examples for how to use these structures.

Unit Review Here you'll have a chance to practice what you've learned.

Challenge
Extend your knowledge even further with a challenge activity.

Internet Activity

- Internet activities take you to **www.berlitzbooks.com/5minute**, where you can test drive your new language skills. Just look for the computer symbol.

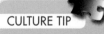
5-Minute Spanish audio
When you see this symbol, you'll know to listen to the specified track on the *5-Minute Spanish* audio CD.

SMART TIP
Boxes like these are here to extend your Spanish knowledge. You'll find differences in Spanish from country to country, extra language conventions and other helpful information on how to speak better Spanish.

CULTURE TIP
Boxes like these introduce useful cultural information about Spanish-speaking countries.

SMART PRONUNCIATION
Boxes like these demonstrate specific pronunciation tools. For example, did you know that in some countries the letter *d* is pronounced with a lisp, while in others it's pronounced with a normal *d* sound? You'll learn more as you move further along in the book.

This section is designed to make you familiar with the sounds of Spanish using our simplified phonetic transcription. You'll find the pronunciation of the Spanish letters and sounds explained below, together with their "imitated" equivalents. Simply read the pronunciation as if it were English, noting any special rules below.

The acute accent ´ indicates stress, e.g. *río*, <u>ree</u>·oh. Some Spanish words have more than one meaning. In these instances, the accent mark is also used to distinguish between them, e.g.: *él* (he) and *el* (the); *sí* (yes) and *si* (if).

Consonants

Letter	Approximate Pronunciation	Example	Pronunciation
b	1. as in English b	**bueno**	<u>bweh</u>·noh
	2. between vowels as in English, but softer	**bebida**	beh·<u>bee</u>·dah
c	1. before e and i like s in same	**centro**	<u>sehn</u>·troh
	2. otherwise like k in kit	**como**	<u>koh</u>·moh
g	1. before e and i, like ch in Scottish loch	**urgente**	oor·<u>khehn</u>·teh
	2. otherwise, like g in get	**ninguno**	neen·<u>goo</u>·noh
h	always silent	**hombre**	<u>ohm</u>·breh
j	like ch in Scottish loch	**bajo**	<u>bah</u>·khoh
ll	like y in yellow	**lleno**	<u>yeh</u>·noh
ñ	like ni in onion	**señor**	seh·<u>nyohr</u>
q	like k in kick	**quince**	<u>keen</u>·seh
r	trilled, especially at the beginning of a word	**río**	<u>ree</u>·oh
rr	strongly trilled	**arriba**	ah·<u>rree</u>·bah
s	1. like s in same	**sus**	soos
	2. before b, d, g, l, m, n, like s in rose	**mismo**	<u>meez</u>·moh
v	like b in bad, but softer	**viejo**	<u>beeyeh</u>·khoh
z	like s in same	**brazo**	<u>brah</u>·soh

Letters ch, d, f, k, l, m, n, p, t, w, x and y are pronounced as in English.

Vowels

Letter	Approximate Pronunciation	Example	Pronunciation
a	like the a in father	**gracias**	<u>grah</u>·seeyahs
e	like e in get	**esta**	<u>ehs</u>·tah
i	like ee in meet	**sí**	see
o	like o in rope	**dos**	dohs
u	1. like oo in food 2. silent after g and q 3. when marked ü, like we in well	**uno** **que** **antigüedad**	<u>oo</u>·noh keh ahn·tee·gweh·<u>dahd</u>
y	1. like y in yellow 2. when alone, like ee in meet 3. when preceded by an a, sounds like y + ee, with ee faintly pronounced	**hoy** **y** **hay**	oy ee aye

Below are some major consonant differences you'll hear in the Spanish spoken in Spain as opposed to most countries in Latin America.

Letter	Approximate Pronunciation	Example	Pronunciation
c	1. before e and i like th in thin 2. otherwise like k in kit	**centro** **como**	<u>then</u>·troh <u>koh</u>·moh
d	1. as in English 2. between vowels and especially at the end of a word, like th in thin, but softer	**donde** **usted**	<u>dohn</u>·deh oos·<u>teth</u>
z	like th in thin	**brazo**	<u>brah</u>·thoh

In this unit you will:
- learn common phrases to greet and say goodbye.
- say your name and where you are from.
- learn personal pronouns and two uses of the verb *ser* (to be).
- learn common phrases and words about nationality.

LESSON 1

¡Buenos días!

Dialogue

Lisa meets her new neighbor Marco. Listen as she introduces herself and asks Marco where he is from.

Lisa Buenos días. Me llamo Lisa. ¿Cómo se llama usted?

Marco Me llamo Marco. Mucho gusto.

Lisa Soy de España. Y usted, ¿de dónde es?

Marco Soy de México.

Lisa Encantada.

Marco Igualmente. Hasta luego.

SMART TIP

In most Spanish conversations, speakers will drop the personal pronoun. For example, instead of *Yo soy de España*, you may say *Soy de España*.

Activity A

Circle **T** for true and **F** for false.

1 This meeting happens during the day. **T / F**
2 Marco is happy to meet Lisa. **T / F**
3 Lisa is from the Dominican Republic. **T / F**
4 Marco is from Mexico. **T / F**

Activity B

Fill in the missing questions or statements with phrases from the dialogue.

Me llamo Lisa. ¿ _____?

Me llamo Marco. _____.

Soy de España. Y usted, ¿ _____?

Soy _____.

CULTURE TIP

In most Spanish-speaking countries, friends and family members usually say hello with a kiss or a hug. In Spain you need two kisses, one on each cheek. In Mexico a kiss or a hug will do.

Encantada.

Encantado.

Core Phrases

¡Hola!	Hello!
¡Adiós! or Hasta luego.	Goodbye!
Buenos días.	Good morning.
Buenas tardes.	Good afternoon.
Buenas noches.	Good night.
¿Cómo se llama usted?	What is your name?
¿De dónde es usted?	Where are you from?

Extra Phrases

¿Cómo está?	How are you?
Encantado/Encantada or Mucho gusto.	Nice to meet you.
Igualmente.	Likewise.

Activity A

What do you say if you want to…

1   …say hello?

_____

2   …ask someone his/her name?

_____

3   …ask someone where he/she is from?

_____

4   …say goodbye?

_____

Activity B

For each picture write the appropriate Spanish greeting: *Buenos días, Buenas tardes* or *Buenas noches*.

1   _____

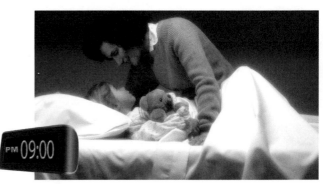

2   _____

3   _____

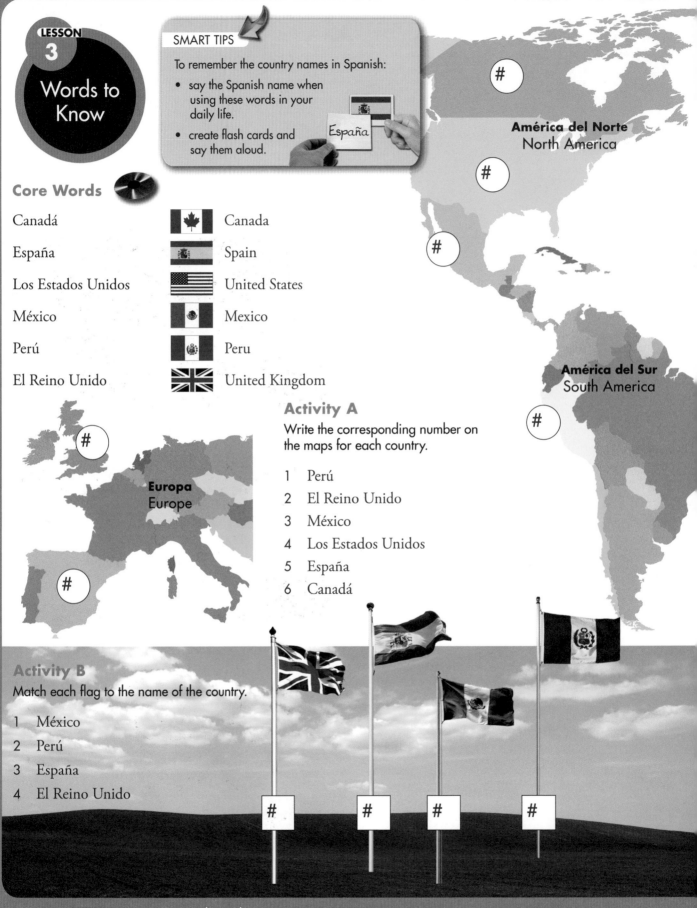

SMART TIPS

To remember the country names in Spanish:

• say the Spanish name when using these words in your daily life.

• create flash cards and say them aloud.

España

Core Words

Canadá		Canada
España		Spain
Los Estados Unidos		United States
México		Mexico
Perú		Peru
El Reino Unido		United Kingdom

América del Norte
North America

#

#

#

América del Sur
South America

#

Europa
Europe

#

#

Activity A

Write the corresponding number on the maps for each country.

1 Perú
2 El Reino Unido
3 México
4 Los Estados Unidos
5 España
6 Canadá

Activity B

Match each flag to the name of the country.

1 México
2 Perú
3 España
4 El Reino Unido

#   #   #   #

Smart Grammar

Personal Pronouns

yo	I
tú	you (inf.)
usted	you (form.)
él/ella	he/she
nosotros/nosotras	we (m/f)
ustedes	you (pl.)
ellos/ellas	they (m/f)

Abbreviations

masculine	m	singular	sing.	informal	inf.
feminine	f	plural	pl.	formal	form.

Activity A

Write the correct singular pronoun under each picture.

1 _____
I

2 _____
she

3 _____
he

4 _____
you (inf.)

Activity B

Write the correct plural pronoun under each picture.

1 _____
they

2 _____
they

3 _____
we

4 _____
we

Activity C

Write the pronoun you use when talking about…

1 …yourself.   _____

2 …a woman.   _____

3 …a man.   _____

4 …a group of women. _____

5 …a group of men.   _____

> **SMART TIPS**
>
> - Use the masculine plural pronoun if there is at least one male in the group.
> - In most regions of Spain, *vosotros/vosotras* is the personal pronoun for "you," plural. This pronoun and its verbal forms are used instead of *ustedes*.

¿De dónde eres?

Idioma y nacionalidad

El español es el idioma oficial de 21 países en el mundo. Algunos de estos países son España, México, Colombia, Argentina, Perú y Ecuador. Cada país en el que se habla español tiene su propia nacionalidad. Así como alguien de Canadá es canadiense, no inglés, alguien de Perú es peruano, no español. Esta tabla muestra otros ejemplos de países, nacionalidades y sus idiomas.

País	Nacionalidad	Idioma
Argentina	argentina	español
Colombia	colombiana	español
Ecuador	ecuatoriana	español
España	española	español
México	mexicana	español
República Dominicana	dominicana	español

Language and Nationality

Spanish is the official language of 21 countries in the world. Some of those countries are Spain, Mexico, Colombia, Argentina, Peru and Ecuador. Each Spanish-speaking country has its own nationality. Just as someone from Canada is Canadian, not English, someone from Peru is Peruvian, not Spanish. The table above shows other examples of countries, nationalities and languages.

Where are you from?

Read the article about Spanish-speaking countries and nationalities—don't worry if you can't understand every word, but try to get the gist of the story. Underline the Spanish words that are familiar or similar to any words in English. Then read the English translation.

Activity A

Complete the bilingual chart with words from the article. The first one is done for you.

country	país
language	
nationality	
Spanish	
English	

Activity B

Cover the English translation of the article. Read the Spanish article again and circle the correct answer.

1 Spanish is the official language in 21
   a países   b idiomas

2 People in Colombia speak
   a colombiano   b español

3 Someone from Canada is
   a inglés   b canadiense

4 Someone from Peru is
   a español   b peruano

> **SMART TIP**
>
> Words for nationality and language are not capitalized in Spanish unless they are at the beginning of a sentence. For example, in English we write "I am **M**exican. I speak **S**panish." In Spanish, we write *Soy* **m**exicano. Hablo **e**spañol.

LESSON 6
Words to Know

Core Words

australiano/australiana	Australian (m/f)
inglés/inglesa	English (m/f)
canadiense	Canadian
español/española	Spanish (m/f)
estadounidense	American
mexicano/mexicana	Mexican (m/f)

Extra Words

alemán/alemana	German (m/f)
francés/francesa	French (m/f)
irlandés/irlandesa	Irish (m/f)
italiano/italiana	Italian (m/f)
portugués/portuguesa	Portuguese (m/f)

Activity A

Choose the correct nationality for each person.

1 (Mexican) Teresa es _____.
mexicana/española

2 (American) Sarah es _____.
inglesa/estadounidense

3 (English) Tim es _____.
inglés/canadiense

4 (Australian) Matthew es _____.
australiano/peruano

Activity B

Use the vocabulary from the word box to identify each dish's nationality.

> canadiense   inglesa   estadounidense
> española   mexicana

1 _____

2 _____

3 _____

4 _____

5 _____

SMART TIP

Most adjectives in Spanish have a masculine and feminine form. For example, "Mexican" is either *mexicano* (m) or *mexicana* (f). A man says *Soy mexicano.* A woman says *Soy mexicana.* In Activity B, the feminine forms *inglesa, española* and *mexicana* are used because you were identifying the food's *nacionalidad* (nationality).

Smart Phrases

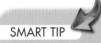

SMART TIP

The masculine forms of the adjectives "English" and "Spanish," *inglés* and *español,* are also the words for the languages. For example, an English man would say *Soy inglés* (I am English) and *Hablo inglés* (I speak English). An English woman would say *Soy inglesa* and *Hablo inglés.*

Core Phrases

¿Es usted inglés/inglesa?	Are you English?
Soy canadiense.	I'm Canadian.
¿Habla español?	Do you speak Spanish?
Un poco.	A little.
Hablo bien/mal.	I speak well/poorly.

Activity A

What do you say if you want to…

1   …ask someone if he's Spanish?

_____

2   …say you speak a language well?

_____

3   …say you speak a little?

_____

Your Turn

Imagine you just met someone while traveling in Spain. Use the phrases and vocabulary you've learned to create a dialogue. Ask about the person's nationality and the language he/she speaks. Write your questions in the You column. Write the answers in the Person From Spain column.

You	Person From Spain
Q1	A1
Q2	A2

CULTURE TIP

In some Spanish-speaking countries people tend to use the diminutive when they are referring to small quantities. For example, if someone speaks a little English, he/she might say *un poquito* instead of *un poco.*

LESSON 8
Smart Grammar

The verb *ser* (to be)
The verb *ser* has several uses, including:

- introducing yourself or another person

- telling where a person is from and the person's nationality

Singular

yo	soy	I am
tú	eres	you are
usted	es	you are
él/ella	es	he/she is

Examples

Yo soy Lisa.	I am Lisa.
Él es Raúl.	He is Raúl.

Activity A
Fill in the blanks with the correct form of the verb *ser*.

1 Yo _____ de España.

2 Usted _____ de México.

3 Tú _____ de Perú.

4 Ella _____ de Canadá.

SMART TIPS

- In Spanish, the adjective usually agrees with the subject in gender (masculine or feminine) and number. Endings change between masculine and feminine and between singular and plural. For example:
  Pedro es mexicano.
  Pedro y Carlos son mexicanos.
  María es inglesa.
  María y Cristina son inglesas.

- In Spain some people use the pronoun *vosotros/vosotras*. To conjugate the verb *ser* with this pronoun, you would use *sois*. So you would ask *¿Sois españoles?* (Are you Spanish?)

Plural

nosotros/nosotras	somos	we are
ustedes	son	you are
ellos/ellas	son	they are

Examples

Nosotros somos de Perú.	We are from Peru.
Nosotros somos peruanos.	We are Peruvian.

Activity B
Fill in the blanks with the correct form of the verb *ser*.

1 Ustedes _____ estadounidenses.

2 Nosotros _____ mexicanas.

3 Ellos _____ españoles.

4 Ellas _____ inglesas.

Your Turn
Greta, Diego and Paola are getting to know each other. Complete their conversation with the correct form of the verb *ser*.

Diego (to Greta) ¿De dónde _____?

Greta (to Diego and Paola) _____ del Reino Unido. Y ustedes, ¿_____ españoles?

Diego _____ español y Paola _____ mexicana.

Activity A

Complete the following chart.

Nombre	País	Nacionalidad
Pepa		española
Pablo	México	
Cassandra		canadiense
Brian	Los Estados Unidos	
Katie		inglesa

Activity B

Using the verb *ser*, write a complete sentence saying where each person is from.

Example Paulina, El Reino Unido:
Paulina es inglesa.

1 tú, Los Estados Unidos:_____

2 Lisa, España: _____

3 usted, Canadá: _____

4 Ernesto, México: _____

Activity C

Kiko is visiting Mexico. Complete the dialogue as he speaks with his *guía turístico* (tourist guide).

Guía ¡_____! ¡Bienvenido a México!

Kiko ¡Hola! _____ Kiko Buxó. ¿_____
_____ usted?

Guía _____ Enrico. Mucho gusto.

Kiko Encantado. ¿_____ usted mexicano?

Guía Sí. ¿_____?

Kiko _____ del Reino Unido. ¿_____
_____?

Guía Un poquito.

Kiko Hablo _____ y _____.

Guía ¡Qué bien!

Kiko _____, Enrico.

Guía ¡Adiós!

Activity D

Find the countries and the nationalities from the box in the word search. They may be written forward, backward, upside down or diagonally.

> España   Canadá   México   española
> El Reino Unido   Los Estados Unidos   canadiense

```
L  O  S  E  S  T  A  D  O  S  U  N  I  D  O  S
Á  Y  P  I  O  S  U  R  N  C  N  A  S  P  L  B
D  A  A  T  L  E  S  P  A  Ñ  A  D  H  A  E  O
A  L  O  Ñ  A  P  S  E  U  D  I  T  W  P  O  C
N  V  N  I  K  L  T  Ú  R  E  P  C  Z  D  E  I
A  U  C  A  N  A  D  I  E  N  S  E  Y  L  H  X
C  F  D  R  T  U  A  I  P  E  N  W  R  O  U  É
E  L  R  E  I  N  O  U  N  I  D  O  S  Ú  D  M
```

Challenge

Can you find the Spanish terms for *Peru* and *Peruvian* in the word search? Write them below.

Peru _____

Peruvian _____

Activity E

Correct the error in each sentence. Write the correct version of the sentence on the line provided.

1 ¡Adiós! Me llamo Laura. _____

2 Nosotros son de Canadá. _____

3 Pepinot es de España. Pepinot es peruano.
_____

4 Manuel es de estadounidense.
_____

5 Yo hablo canadiense. _____

6 Ana es mexicano. _____

Internet Activity

Are you interested in learning more Spanish names? Go to **www.berlitzbooks.com/5minute** for a list of sites with Spanish names. Browse and pick three or four names you like. Practice saying those names. Try saying *Me llamo...* in front of each one.

Unit 2 Nouns and Numbers

In this unit you will:

- use vocabulary for people, animals and things, and the numbers 1–30.
- learn the differences between masculine and feminine, and singular and plural nouns.
- use the definite articles and regular –ar and –ir verbs.
- practice filling in a form with information about yourself.
- learn how to ask for a telephone number and an address.

LESSON 1

La tarjeta postal

A Postcard from Colombia

Look at the front and back of *la tarjeta postal* (the postcard). Read the text, then circle the words that name people, things or animals.

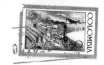

Querida Rosa,

...m having a great time in Colombia, and I'm finally ...arning some Spanish. Look at this picture! ¡Mira la ...to! Mira los animales. There are gatos, perros y pájaros. ...Mira a la gente! There are niños, niñas, hombres y ...ujeres. This is a very nice place. I like the casas and ...dificios very much. Mira los carros y los autobuses. ...hey are so colorful! This foto shows you las personas, los ...nimales y las cosas I'm seeing.

...miss you. Te extraño.
...s: How's my español?

Robert

Ms. Rosa Seurat
Box 219
Anaheim, California
U. S. A.

Activity A

Circle **T** for true and **F** for false.

1 Robert is visiting Spain.		T / F
2 Robert's postcard describes mountains and rivers.		T / F
3 Robert likes the houses and buildings.		T / F
4 The postcard describes colorful cars and buses.		T / F

Activity B

Write the Spanish words that name…

1 …people in the postcard.

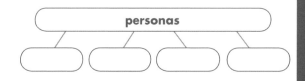

> personas

2 …things in the postcard.

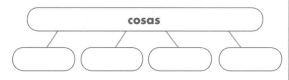

> cosas

3 …animals in the postcard.

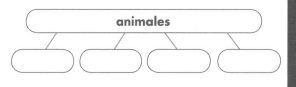

> animales

Extension Activity

If you know more words for people, animals and things add them to the word webs above.

> **SMART TIP**
>
> Notice how all the words for people, animals and things in the postcard end with an –s or –es. This is because they are all in the plural form. The singular forms of the words are: *gato, perro, pájaro, niña, niño, hombre, mujer, casa, edificio, carro* and *autobús*.

Words to Know

Core Words

la niña — girl
el niño — boy
el hombre — man
la mujer — woman

el pájaro — bird
el gato — cat
el perro — dog

el autobús — bus
el carro — car

la calle — street
la casa — house
el edificio — building

Activity A

Write the Spanish word for each item in the pictures.

1

2

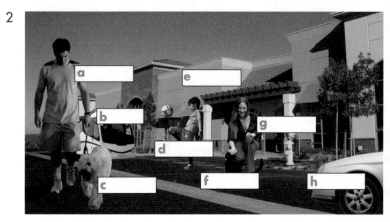

Activity B

Write *femenino* (feminine) or *masculino* (masculine) to classify each noun.

1 perro _____
2 niño _____
3 carro _____
4 calle _____
5 edificio _____
6 casa _____
7 gato _____
8 autobús _____

Smart Phrases

Core Phrases

¡Mira a la gente!	Look at the people!
¡Mira los animales!	Look at the animals!
Querido/Querida _____.	Dear _____. (m/f)
Te extraño.	I miss you.

SMART TIPS

- *¡Mira este consejo!* (Look at this tip!) When you refer to people or a specific animal in Spanish, you should use the preposition *a* after the phrase *¡Mira...!* and before the noun. For example: *¡Mira a Laura! ¡Mira a Rover! ¡Mira a los niños!* When you refer to animals or things in general, you should drop the preposition *a* and say *¡Mira los animales!*

- If you want to be formal in your conversation, use *¡Mire...!* instead of *¡Mira...!*

Activity A

Laura is walking with Ernesto. As they walk, she points at people and things. Write a phrase in each speech balloon to indicate what Laura shows Ernesto.

1 _____
_____

2 _____
_____

Activity B

Fill in the blanks in Spanish to help Laura write a postcard to her friend.

PRIMER DIA
DE SERVICIO

COLOMBIA

_____ Elena,

I'm having a great time here, and I'm learning

some _____.   i_____ a la gente!

There are _____, _____ y _____.

¡Mira las _____! ¡Mira el _____! i_____

los animales! There are _____, _____ y _____.

Te _____.

Laura

LESSON 4
Smart Grammar

Singular and Plural Nouns

There are four basic rules to forming plural nouns:

- add –s when the noun ends in a vowel: *casa/casas* (house/houses).
- add –es when the noun ends in a consonant that is not –z: *túnel/túneles* (tunnel/tunnels).
- if the noun ends in –z, drop the –z and replace it with –ces; *luz/luces* (light/lights).
- in general, when a singular noun has an accent on the last syllable, drop the accent for the plural form: *canción/canciones* (song/songs).

Activity A

Write the plural form of the nouns.

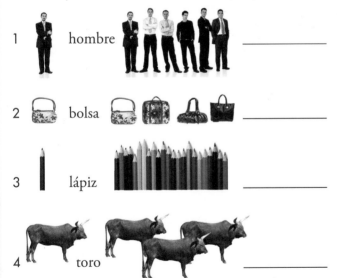

1   hombre   _____

2   bolsa   _____

3   lápiz   _____

4   toro   _____

Definite Articles

The definite article in Spanish varies with the gender and number of the noun.

el   (m, sing.)
la   (f, sing.)
los   (m, pl.)
las   (f, pl.)

SMART TIP

Although *agua* (water) is a feminine noun, you must use the masculine definite article: *el agua*. The purpose is to avoid pronouncing two *a*'s together. This is true for some other words beginning with an *a* sound, such as *águila* (eagle) and *hambre* (hunger).

Activity B

Write the correct definite article next to each noun.

1   _____   niño
2   _____   calle
3   _____   perros
4   _____   mujeres
5   _____   lápiz
6   _____   autobús

Activity C

Look at the pictures and write the corresponding nouns with the correct definite articles.

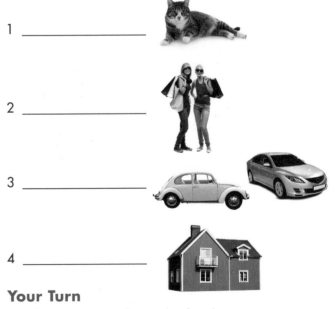

1   _____

2   _____

3   _____

4   _____

Your Turn

See if you can guess the article of each new noun.

1   _____ puerta (door)
2   _____ cartas (letters)
3   _____ papel (paper)
4   _____ barcos (ships)
5   _____ basura (trash)

Passport / Landing card images

Signature: Jennifer Jameson

UNITED STATES OF AMERICA

Type / Type / Tipo Code / Code / Código Passport No / No du Passeport / No de Pasaporte
P USA 98765234500

Surname / Nom / Apellidos
JAMESON

Given Names / Prénoms / Nombres
JENNIFER K

Nationality / Nationalité / Nacionalidad
UNITED STATES OF AMERICA

Date of birth / Date de naissance / Fecha de nacimiento
6/30/78

Place of birth / Lieu de naissance / Lugar de nacimiento
27 MAIN ST AKRON OHIO 44313

Sex / Sexe / Sexo
F

Date of issue / Date de délivrance / Fecha de expedición
2007

Authority / Autorité / Autoridad
United States
Department of State

Date of expiration / Date d'expiration / Fecha de caducidad
2017

Endorsements / Mentions Spéciales / Anotaciones
SEE PAGE 27

USA

P<USAJAMESON<<JENNIFER<<<<<<<<<<<<<<<<<<<<<<<<<<

BIENVENIDOS AL PERU
DECLARACION JURADA DE EQUIPAJES
Tarjeta de imigración

Apellido(s) Jameson	Nombre(s) Jennifer K.	Sexo F
Fecha de nacimiento día: 30 mes: 06 año: 1978	Profesión estudiante	Nacionalidad estadounidense
Lugar de nacimiento Calle Main	Número 27	Ciudad Akron
Provincia/Estado Ohio		Código Postal 44313
País Estados Unidos	Teléfono 1-730-555-2018	
Dirección en Perú Avenida Ricardo Palma 955, Miraflores, Lima 18, Perú.		

Jennifer K. Jameson
Firma

27-12-09
Fecha

Student Identification

Jennifer is on a plane going to Lima, Peru. Compare her passport to her landing card.

Activity A

Match the Spanish word with its English equivalent.

1	dirección	a	date of birth
2	calle	b	last name
3	apellido	c	address
4	fecha de nacimiento	d	street

CULTURE TIP

Outside the U.S., the date is usually written as day/month/year. So June 30, 2009 would be 30/06/09. When writing an address, the house or building number often comes after the street name. For example, 987 Washington Avenue is *Avenida Washington 987*.

Activity B

Jennifer will be studying Spanish at a school in Lima. Use the information above to complete the address section of her application.

FORMA DE ADMISIONES

Universidad de las Lenguas

Dirección en Perú:

Número: _____

Calle: _____

Ciudad: _____ Estado: _____

LESSON 6
Words to Know

Core Words
Los números (Numbers)

uno	1	doce	12
dos	2	trece	13
tres	3	catorce	14
cuatro	4	quince	15
cinco	5	dieciséis	16
seis	6	diecisiete	17
siete	7	dieciocho	18
ocho	8	diecinueve	19
nueve	9	veinte	20
diez	10	treinta	30
once	11		

Datos personales (Personal Information)

la avenida	avenue
la calle	street
la dirección	address
el teléfono	telephone

Activity A

Identify the pattern in the words *dieciséis, diecisiete* and *veintiuno, veintidós, veintitrés.* Then write the Spanish words to complete the number sequences.

quince, dieciséis, diecisiete, _____, _____, veinte

veintiuno, veintidós, veintitrés, _____, _____, _____, _____, _____, _____, treinta

Activity B

Read the numbers 1–30 aloud in Spanish. Then match each number with the correct word below.

1	diez	**4**	doce
6	uno	**9**	quince
13	treinta	**12**	catorce
18	seis	**15**	cuatro
10	trece	**22**	veintidós
30	dieciocho	**14**	nueve

Activity C

Translate the following information from Spanish to English.

1 Calle catorce

_____

2 Ave. Margarita, número veintisiete

_____

3 Tel. uno-siete-ocho, tres-siete-cinco, cuatro-dos-uno-nueve

_____

4 C.P. uno-uno-nueve-dos-seis

_____

SMART TIP

Watch out for these common abbreviations in Spanish:

avenida	Ave.
número	No.
código postal	C.P.
teléfono	Tel.

Consulado
No. 29
Ave. Aduana, Madrid, C.P. 28070
Tel. 914 617 585

CULTURE TIP

In Spain and some other Spanish-speaking countries, you use *el teléfono móvil* instead of *el teléfono celular* when referring to cellular or mobile phones.

LESSON 7

Smart Phrases

Core Phrases

¿Cuál es su número de teléfono?	What's your phone number?
¿Cuál es su dirección?	What's your address?
¿Cuál es su fecha de nacimiento?	When's your birthday?
Mi dirección es ___.	My address is ___.
Mi fecha de nacimiento es ___.	My birthday is ___.
Mi teléfono es ___.	My phone number is ___.
¿Dónde vive?	Where do you live?

> **SMART TIP**
>
> To ask for someone's e-mail, just say *¿Cuál es su dirección de correo electrónico?* To answer, say *Mi dirección de correo electrónico es…*

Activity A

Write your *nombre, fecha de nacimiento, dirección* and *número de teléfono* in Spanish.

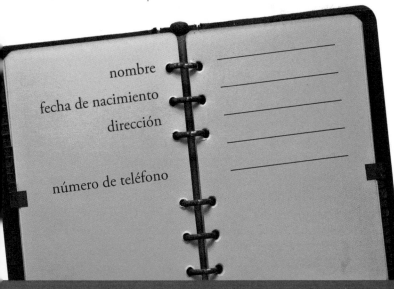

nombre

fecha de nacimiento

dirección

número de teléfono

Activity B

What is Karina asking Pedro? Circle the correct answer.

1

¿Dónde vive?

a the place where he lives
b the place where he works

2

¿Cuál es su dirección?

a the place where he lives
b his phone number

3

¿Cuál es su número de teléfono?

a his phone number
b his date of birth

4

¿Cuál es su fecha de nacimiento?

a his phone number
b his date of birth

Smart Grammar

Regular Verbs in the Present Tense

Regular verbs in Spanish end in *–ar, –er* or *–ir* in the infinitive. Look at the chart to see how to conjugate verbs in the present tense with *–ar* and *–ir*. You will learn verbs with *–er* in the next unit.

Verbs with *–ar*

Drop the *–ar* and add the appropriate ending for each pronoun, such as with *estudiar* (to study).

yo	estud**io**	I study
tú	estud**ias**	you study
usted	estud**ia**	you study
él/ella	estud**ia**	he/she studies
nosotros/nosotras	estud**iamos**	we study
ustedes	estud**ian**	you study
ellos/ellas	estud**ian**	they study

Examples Yo estudio.   I study.
        Nosotros estudiamos.   We study.

Activity A

Conjugate the verb *estudiar* in the present tense.

yo   _____
tú   _____
él/ella   _____
usted   _____
nosotros/nosotras _____
ustedes   _____
ellos/ellas   _____

SMART TIP

When you name a series of things you can use the conjunction *y* (and): *Estudio francés, inglés y español* (I study French, English and Spanish).

Verbs with *–ir*

Drop the *–ir* and add the appropriate ending for each pronoun, such as with *vivir* (to live).

yo	viv**o**	I live
tú	viv**es**	you live
usted	viv**e**	you live
él/ella	viv**e**	he/she lives
nosotros/nosotras	viv**imos**	we live
ustedes	viv**en**	you live
ellos/ellas	viv**en**	they live

Examples Tú vives.   You live. (sing.)
        Ustedes viven.   You live. (pl.)

Activity B

Conjugate the verb *vivir* in the present tense.

yo   _____
tú   _____
él/ella   _____
usted   _____
nosotros/nosotras _____
ustedes   _____
ellos/ellas   _____

Activity C

Look at the pictures. Write in Spanish where each person lives. Be sure to use the appropriate conjugation of *vivir*.

Tomás, 10 Orchard Street

_____

Julia and Max, 24 7th Street

_____

Carmen and I, 16 Main Street

_____

Your Turn

Think about the verb *enseñar* (to teach). How would you say in Spanish that you teach English and Spanish? How would you say that Marissa teaches English?

Activity A

How many of each do you see? Use the correct plural form when necessary.

1 _____

2 _____

3 _____

4 _____

Activity B

Use the address book to answer the following questions. Remember that in Spanish the order of some words may change.

Javier Colón 25 Huron Street	482 913 7391
Eduardo González 15 Columbia Street	+44 828 227 1984
Andrea Rodríguez 8 4th Avenue	+44 20 2278 3625
Corrine & Mark Smith 30 4th Street	716 548 3549

1 ¿Dónde vive Andrea?

2 ¿Cuál es el número de teléfono de Javier? (use the word form)

3 ¿Dónde viven Corrine y Mark?

4 ¿Cuál es el número de teléfono de Andrea?

5 ¿Dónde vive Javier?

Activity C

Look at each noun and write the correct article. Don't forget to think about the number and gender of each noun. Then say a phrase with ¡Mira...! to show each item or items.

1 _____ pájaros

2 _____ mujeres

3 _____ autobús

4 _____ dirección

> **Challenge**
>
> Use a dictionary to look up *caminar* and *sufrir*. Write two sentences for each verb using the pronouns *él* and *ellos*.

Activity D

You've just arrived at the Sancho Language Institute's office to study Spanish. Laura, the receptionist, needs some basic information. She doesn't understand English, so you must respond in Spanish. Complete the conversation.

Laura ¡Hola! ¿Cómo se llama?

Usted _____

Laura Bien, ¿cuál es su número de teléfono?

Usted _____

Laura ¿Cuál es su dirección?

Usted _____

Laura ¿Y el código postal?

Usted _____

Laura Por último, ¿cuál es su fecha de nacimiento?

Usted _____

Laura ¡Excelente! Bienvenido al Instituto de Idiomas Sancho.

Usted _____

Internet Activity

Go to **www.berlitzbooks.com/5minute** for a list of map-related websites with satellite features in Spanish. When you find one, type in the address for the Instituto Cervantes: Alcalá, 49 28014 Madrid. Zoom in on the map. If you studied Spanish at the Instituto Cervantes, where would you want to stay?

Unit 3   Time and Date

In this unit you will:

- tell *la hora* (the time) and *la fecha* (the date).
- learn the numbers 31 and up.
- conjugate regular *–er* verbs.
- learn the irregular verb *hacer* (to do).

LESSON
1

¿Qué hora es?

Dialogue

Diana and Juan are watching a soccer game. Listen to them talk about the time, how much time is left, how long the game is and the score.

Diana ¿Qué hora es?

Juan Son las seis y treinta y cinco.

Diana ¡Es temprano! ¿Cuánto tiempo falta en el juego?

Juan Faltan cincuenta y cinco minutos. El juego dura noventa minutos.

Diana ¿Cuál es el marcador?

Juan Rayados 1, Blancos 0.

Activity A

Write the correct answer in Spanish.

1   What time is it?

_____

2   How much time is left in the game?

_____

3   How long is the game?

_____

4   Which team is winning?

_____

Activity B

Put the dialogue in order.
Number the phrases 1–4.

¡Es temprano! ¿Cuánto tiempo falta en el juego?

#

Son las seis y treinta y cinco.

#

Faltan cincuenta y cinco minutos.

#

¿Qué hora es?

#

CULTURE TIP

In Spain, like most parts of Europe, the time is read according to the 24-hour clock. For example, 6:35 PM (*seis y treinta y cinco*) is 18:35 (*dieciocho y treinta y cinco*). In most parts of Latin America the time is read according to the 12-hour clock.

Smart Phrases

Core Phrases

¿Qué hora es?	What time is it?
Son las dos de la mañana.	It's 2 AM.
Es la una de la mañana.	It's 1 AM.
Son las dos de la tarde.	It's 2 PM.
Son las diez de la noche.	It's 10 PM.
Son las siete y media.	It's 7:30.
Son las seis y cuarto.	It's a quarter after 6.
Son las siete menos cuarto.	It's a quarter to 7.
¡Es tarde!	It's late!
¡Es temprano!	It's early!

Activity A

Look at the clock and write a sentence telling what time it is.

Example

Son las siete y cuarto.

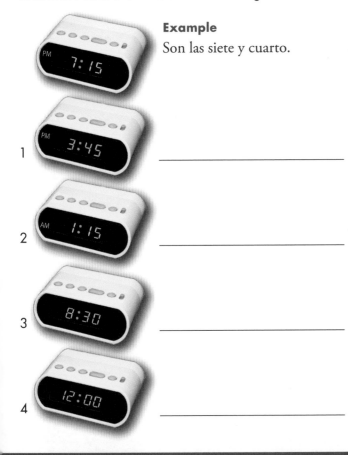

1 _____

2 _____

3 _____

4 _____

Activity B

You are supposed to meet a friend at *ocho en punto* (8:00 PM sharp). Look at the time and tell whether it is early or late. Write *¡Es temprano!* or *¡Es tarde!*

1 Son las siete menos cuarto. _____

2 Son las ocho y cuarto. _____

3 Son las siete y media. _____

4 Son las nueve. _____

Activity C

What do you say if you want to…

1 …ask for the time?

_____

2 …say it's early?

_____

3 …say it's late?

_____

4 …say it's 2 AM?

_____

SMART TIP

There are several ways to say the time when it's 45 minutes past the hour. For example, at 5:45 you can say *Son las cinco y cuarenta y cinco* (It's 5 and 40 and 5), *Son las seis menos un cuarto* (It's 6 minus a quarter) or *Son cuarto para las seis* (It's a quarter to 6).

LESSON 3

Words to Know

Core Words

El tiempo (Time)

la hora	hour
el minuto	minute
el segundo	second
en punto	o'clock sharp

Los números (Numbers)

treinta y uno	thirty-one
treinta y dos	thirty-two
treinta y tres	thirty-three
treinta y cuatro	thirty-four
treinta y cinco	thirty-five
cuarenta	forty
cincuenta	fifty
sesenta	sixty

Extra Words

la media	half
el cuarto	quarter

SMART TIP

Did you notice the pattern in numbers 31–35? Numbers that are between the tens (30, 40, 50, etc.) follow a pattern: 31 is *treinta y uno* (thirty and one), and so on. Can you guess what 36–40 are in Spanish?

Activity A

Write the following numbers in word form.

1 44 _____

2 32 _____

3 67 _____

4 58 _____

Activity B

¿Cuánto tiempo falta? A show starts at *las ocho en punto.* How much time is left until the show? Write the time in word form. Use *falta* for singular and *faltan* for plural. Also be sure to use the plural of *hora* and *minuto* when the answer is more than one.

Example

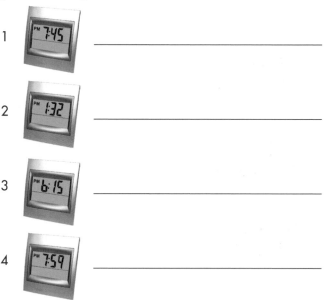

Falta una hora
y quince minutos.

Faltan veinte minutos.

¿Cuánto tiempo falta?

1 _____

2 _____

3 _____

4 _____

Your Turn

It's 4:12 PM and you are watching a soccer game. The first half started at 4 PM and it lasts 45 minutes. You look at the clock every ten minutes.

Tell the time and how many minutes are left in the first half each time you look at the clock. Start at 4:12 PM.

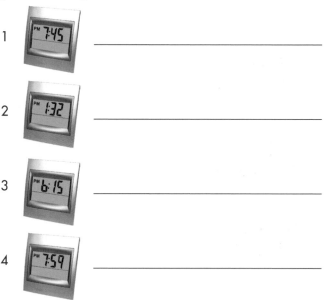

LESSON 4
Smart Grammar

Regular Verbs in the Present Tense

Verbs with –er

To conjugate regular –er verbs such as *ver* (to see), drop the –r and add an ending as follows:

yo	ve**o**	I see
tú	ve**s**	you see
usted	ve	you see
él/ella	ve	he/she sees
nosotros/nosotras	ve**mos**	we see
ustedes	ve**n**	you see
ellos/ellas	ve**n**	they see

Examples	Él ve.	He sees.
	Ellas ven.	They see.

Activity A

Complete the following chart to conjugate the verb *correr* (to run) in the present tense.

yo _____

tú _____

él/ella _____

usted _____

nosotros/nosotras _____

ustedes _____

ellos/ellas _____

Activity B
Write the correct form of each –er verb.

1  `ver`   Yo _____

2 `leer`   Ella _____

3  `comer`   Nosotros _____

4  `correr`   Ellas _____

Your Turn
Describe what is happening in the picture.

`comer`   `beber`   `agua`   `pastel`

_____

_____

Los quehaceres

lavar la ropa

hacer los deberes

barrer el suelo

hacer ejercicio

llamar a Francisco

Things to Do

Julia is thinking about the things she has to do today. Look at the pictures and their labels.

Activity A

Choose the correct answer for each question.

1 What is the first thing Julia has to do?
   a wash clothes   **b do homework**

2 Which word goes with the verb "to sweep"?
   a ropa   **b suelo**

3 Which phrase means "to do homework"?
   a hacer los deberes **b hacer ejercicio**

4 Which word means "things to do"?
   a barrer   **b quehaceres**

5 What will Julia do before she calls Francisco?
   a ejercicio   **b los deberes**

Los quehaceres
lavar la ropa
barrer el suelo
hacer los deberes
llamar a Francisco
hacer ejercicio

SMART TIP

The verb *llamar* (to call) is followed by the preposition *a* before the name of the person who is being called. For example, *Jorge llama a Lola* (Jorge calls Lola).

Activity B

Write the appropriate Spanish chore next to each picture.

1 _____

Rosario
56 896818

2 _____

3 _____

4 _____

Words to Know

Core words

Días de la semana (Days of the Week)

el lunes	Monday
el martes	Tuesday
el miércoles	Wednesday
el jueves	Thursday
el viernes	Friday
el sábado	Saturday
el domingo	Sunday

Meses del año (Months of the Year)

enero	January
febrero	February
marzo	March
abril	April
mayo	May
junio	June
julio	July
agosto	August
septiembre	September
octubre	October
noviembre	November
diciembre	December

SMART TIPS

- In Spanish-speaking countries the date is written by placing the day before the month. So November 10 would be 10/11 or *10 de noviembre.*
- All years in Spanish are expressed as regular numbers. For example: 1999 would be *mil novecientos noventa y nueve* (one thousand nine hundred ninety-nine). 2000 is *dos mil* and 2009 is *dos mil nueve.*
- The names of days and months in Spanish are not capitalized.

Activity A

Look over Ignacio's agenda for the week and answer the questions below.

AGENDA

lunes	hacer ejercicio
martes	barrer el suelo
miércoles	hacer los deberes
jueves	hacer ejercicio
viernes	llamar a Daniela
sábado	hacer los deberes
domingo	lavar la ropa

1 What day will Ignacio sweep the floor? _____

2 What days will Ignacio exercise? _____ y _____

3 What day will Ignacio call Daniela? _____

4 What days will Ignacio do his homework? _____ y _____

5 What day will Ignacio do laundry? _____

Activity B

Write each date in Spanish. Remember: The first number is the day.

Example: Thursday 24/02 ____jueves, 24 de febrero____

1 Monday 17/11 _____

2 Saturday 05/06 _____

3 Wednesday 21/09 _____

4 Friday 08/04 _____

5 Tuesday 31/01 _____

6 Sunday 12/08 _____

7 Thursday 25/03 _____

8 Sunday 14/10 _____

9 Monday 29/05 _____

10 Tuesday 02/12 _____

11 Friday 15/07 _____

12 Wednesday 18/02 _____

Smart Phrases

niño

Core Phrases

¿Qué día es hoy?	What day is today?
Hoy es martes.	Today is Tuesday.
¿Cuál es la fecha de hoy?	What is today's date?
¿En qué mes estamos?	What month is this?
¿En qué año estamos?	What year is this?

Activity A

Circle the best response.

1   ¿Qué día es hoy?

   a   enero   **b   Hoy es martes.**

2   ¿En qué mes estamos?

   a   lunes   **b   diciembre**

3   ¿Cuál es la fecha de hoy?

   a   Hoy es 14 de julio del 2009.   **b   Hoy es miércoles.**

4   ¿En qué año estamos?

   a   23 de agosto   **b   2009**

CULTURE TIP

An important date to remember in most countries and cultures is someone's *cumpleaños* (birthday). In Spain and some Latin American countries, after wishing someone *¡Feliz cumpleaños!* (Happy birthday) it is common to pull on the person's earlobe for each year he/she has been alive. To find out when someone's birthday is, ask: *¿Cuándo es su cumpleaños?*

Activity B

Write the questions to complete the mini-conversations.

1   ¿ _____ ?   Hoy es miércoles.

2   ¿ _____ ?   18 de junio

3   ¿ _____ ?   abril

4   ¿ _____ ?   2010

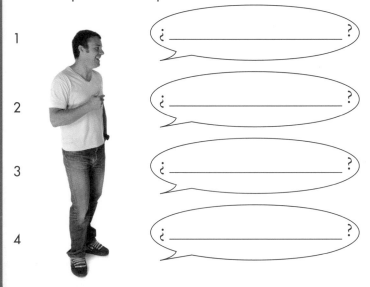

Smart Grammar

The verb *hacer* (to do)

The verb *hacer* is irregular. The chart shows its conjugation in the present tense.

yo	hago	I do
tú	haces	you do
usted	hace	you do
él/ella	hace	he/she does
nosotros/nosotras	hacemos	we do
ustedes	hacen	you do
ellos/ellas	hacen	they do

Activity A

Fill in the blanks with the correct conjugation of *hacer*.

1   Tú _____ ejercicio el lunes.

2   María _____ ejercicio el martes.

3   Carmelo y Lolita _____ ejercicio el miércoles.

4   Isabel y yo _____ ejercicio los jueves.

CULTURE TIPS

- In most Spanish-speaking countries "to do laundry" is *lavar la ropa* (literally, to wash the clothes). In Spain, it's *hacer la colada*.

- "To do homework" can be *hacer los deberes* or *hacer la tarea*. Though often interchangeable, one or the other may be more commonly used depending on the country or region.

Activity B

¿Qué hacen estas personas? Match each picture with a phrase to tell what each person is doing.

1   Él hace café.   _____

2   Ellos hacen un plan.   _____

3   Ella hace un pastel.   _____

Your Turn

Write sentences telling what activities you do on Saturdays and Sundays. Be sure to use the correct form of the verb *hacer*.

_____

_____

_____

_____

_____

_____

_____

Activity A

Choose activities from the box to tell what Irene does at each time. Use the *ella* form of each verb. Don't forget to include *de la mañana, de la tarde* or *de la noche.*

> barrer el suelo   hacer ejercicio   hacer los deberes
> llamar a Pedro   lavar la ropa

1 PM 12:30

Irene hace los deberes a las doce y media de la tarde.

2 PM 8:45

_____

3 PM 6:00

_____

4 AM 7:45

_____

5 AM 11:15

_____

Activity C

Ignacio lost his planner and forgot his schedule for February. Look at the calendar, then answer the questions.

febrero						
lunes	martes	miércoles	jueves	viernes	sábado	domingo
1	**2**	**3** barrer el suelo	**4**	**5**	**6**	**7**
8	**9**	**10**	**11**	**12**	**13** hacer los deberes	**14**
15 llamar a Felipe	**16**	**17**	**18**	**19**	**20**	**21** hacer ejercicio
22	**23** lavar el carro	**24**	**25**	**26**	**27**	**28**

On what dates has Ignacio scheduled his activities? Write out the date in Spanish as day/date/month.

Example sweep the floor

> miércoles, tres de febrero

1 exercise

_____

2 do homework

_____

3 wash the car

_____

4 call Felipe

_____

Activity B

Look at the following times to tell how much time is left in the game.

Example 1:31:02   Falta una hora, treinta y un minutos y dos segundos.

1   2:34:13   _____

2   0:0:27   _____

3   0:12:39   _____

Internet Activity

Imagine you are planning a trip to Peru. Go to **www.berlitzbooks.com/5minute** to browse Spanish-language airfare search engines. Use your knowledge of dates and time in Spanish to search for non-stop flights to Peru. Which flights will get you in on Friday evening? And on Saturday morning?

Challenge

Write a paragraph about a friend. Tell what he or she learns, studies and does.

In this unit you will:
- introduce your immediate family and talk about your relatives.
- use possessive adjectives and demonstrative pronouns.
- use indefinite articles.
- learn the irregular verb *tener* (to have).

LESSON 1

Foto de familia

Pedro

Carla y sus padres

Juan y Mónica

Patricia

Dialogue

Carla and Sam are talking about their families. Listen as Carla shows Sam pictures of her family and tells him who each person is.

Sam ¿Qué tan grande es su familia, Carla?

Carla Somos siete en la familia. Mire nuestras fotos.

Sam ¡Qué bonita familia! Esa es usted y esos son sus padres, ¿verdad?

Carla Ella es mi madre y él es mi padre. Mire esta foto. Esta niña es mi hermana, Patricia.

Sam Y, ¿son estos sus hermanos?

Carla Sí. Este es mi hermano Juan. Él es el mayor. Este es Pedro. Mi hermano menor.

Sam ¿Quién es ésta?

Carla Esta es Mónica, la esposa de Juan.

Activity A

Circle **T** for true or **F** for false.

1 There are fewer than five people in Carla's family. **T/F**

2 Patricia is Carla's sister. **T/F**

3 Carla has three brothers. **T/F**

4 Mónica is Carla's mother. **T/F**

Activity B

Read the following phrases. Circle the picture that illustrates each phrase.

1 Este es mi padre. **a**   **b**

2 Esta es mi hermana. **a**   **b**

3 Esa es mi madre. **a**   **b**

4 Estos son mis hermanos. **a**   **b**

5 Esa es la esposa de Juan. **a**   **b**

CULTURE TIPS

- There are several versions of the words "mother" and "father" in Spanish. Some of them are regional. You can call your mother *madre, mamá, má* or *mami.* You can call your father *padre, papá, pá* or *papi.*

- The most common words for "husband" and "wife" are *esposo* and *esposa,* but you may also hear the words *marido* and *mujer.* These terms are common in official documents and religious weddings.

Words to Know

Core Words

el esposo	husband
la esposa	wife
la familia	family
el hermano	brother
la hermana	sister
los hermanos	brothers/siblings
el hijo	son
la hija	daughter
la madre	mother
el padre	father
los padres	parents

Extra Words

el mayor	oldest
el menor	youngest

Sam's Family Tree

Tomás   Mariana

Sam   Raquel   Pablo

SMART TIPS

There are two ways to talk about possession:

- by using possessive pronouns such as *mi* (my). You will learn these pronouns in Lesson 4.
- by using the definite article + noun (possession) + *de*. For example: *el esposo de María* (María's husband).

Activity A

Look at Sam's family tree. Complete his description. The first one is done for you.

Somos cinco personas en mi ___familia___. Tomás
                                    family

es mi _____ . Mi _____ se
            father   mother

llama Mariana. Raquel es mi _____ .
                                    sister

Pablo es el _____ de Raquel.
                husband

Activity B

Circle the correct word.

1   Sam y Raquel son   **hermanos   padres**.

2   Sam es el   **hermano   padre**   de Raquel.

3   Mariana es la   **madre   padre**   de Sam.

4   Tomás es el   **hijo   padre**   de Sam y Raquel.

5   Mariana y Tomás son los   **hermanos   padres**
    de Sam y Raquel.

6   Sam es el   **esposo   hijo**   de Mariana y Tomás.

7   Raquel es la   **hija   hijo**   de Mariana y Tomás.

8   Sam y Raquel son los **esposos   hijos** de Mariana
    y Tomás.

9   Raquel es la   **esposo   esposa**   de Pablo.

10 Pablo es el   **esposo   hermano**   de Raquel.

Smart Phrases

Core Phrases

¿Qué tan grande es su familia?	How big is your family?
Somos _____ en la familia.	There are _____ of us in the family.
Mi familia es grande/pequeña.	My family is big/small.
¡Qué bonita familia!	What a nice family!
¡Qué familia tan grande/pequeña!	What a big/small family!

Activity A

Put the phrases in order to create a dialogue.

¿Qué tan grande es su familia?

#1

No. Mi familia es pequeña. Somos cuatro personas.

#

Sí, mi familia es grande. Y, ¿es grande su familia?

#

¡Qué familia tan grande!

#

Somos ocho en la familia. Mire esta foto.

#

Activity B

Write a phrase to tell whether each family is big or small.

1 _____

2 _____

3 _____

4 _____

Your Turn

Use your new vocabulary and phrases to talk about your family. Is it big or small? Do you have any siblings? How many?

LESSON 4 — Smart Grammar

Possessive Adjectives

Possessive adjectives always agree in number with the noun to which they refer. The plural form *nuestro/nuestra* (our) also agrees in gender.

Singular	Plural	English
mi	mis	my
tu	tus	your (sing., inf.)
su	sus	his/her/its, your (sing., form.)
nuestro/nuestra	nuestros/nuestras	our (m/f)
su	sus	your (pl.)
su	sus	their

Examples

Él es mi hermano. — He is my brother.
Ellas son sus hermanas. — They are your sisters.
Su familia es grande. — His/Her family is big.
Nuestra madre se llama Karen. — Our mother's name is Karen.

Activity A

Fill in the blanks with the correct possessive adjectives. They may be either singular or plural, depending on the object.

1 Ella es _____ madre. (my)
2 ¿Es él _____ hermano? (your, inf.)
3 _____ familia es pequeña. (your, form.)
4 Ellas son _____ hermanas. (my)
5 ¿Son ellos _____ padres? (your, inf.)
6 Los hombres son _____ hermanos. (your, form.)
7 _____ casa es grande. (our)
8 Los niños son _____ hijos. (our)

Demonstrative Pronouns

Demonstrative pronouns agree in gender and number with the noun to which they refer.

Singular	English	Plural	English
este/esta	this	estos/estas	these
ese/esa	that	esos/esas	those

Activity B

Read the sentences below. Write the letter of the corresponding picture next to each sentence.

1 Estas son mis hijas. _____
2 Ese es mi carro. _____
3 Este es mi padre. _____
4 Esa es mi casa. _____
5 Esta es mi madre. _____
6 Estos son mis padres. _____
7 Esos son mis perros. _____
8 Estos son mis hijos. _____

SMART TIP

In Castilian Spanish (spoken in Spain), *vuestro/vuestra* is the possessive pronoun for the plural "your." It agrees in gender and number with the noun, just like *nuestro/nuestra*.

Árbol de familia

Carmen (abuela) - - - - Gabriel (abuelo)

Catherine (tía) - - - - Esteban (tío)   Luci (madre) - - - - Carlos (padre)

Gustavo (primo)   Adela (prima)   Paulina   Lucas (hermano) - - - - Nadia (cuñada)

Javier (sobrino)   Jacinta (sobrina)

Family Tree

Paulina Marquez has just created a family tree for her records.

Look at the tree and read each relationship aloud.

Activity A

Describe the relationship of each person to Paulina.

1 Gabriel is _____

2 Luci is _____

3 Adela is _____

4 Jacinta is _____

Activity B

Can you tell who's who in Paulina's family? Write the relationship of each person beside his or her picture.

CULTURE TIP

In some Spanish-speaking countries, families tend to stay close together. Sometimes the family—including grandparents, aunts, uncles and cousins—lives nearby and the children do not leave the nest until they get married. Even then, in some cases, they stay together.

1 _____

2 _____

3 _____

4 _____

Words to Know

Core Words

la abuela	grandmother
el abuelo	grandfather
la tía	aunt
el tío	uncle
el primo	cousin (m)
la prima	cousin (f)
el nieto	grandson
la nieta	granddaughter
el sobrino	nephew
la sobrina	niece

Extra Words

el suegro	father-in-law
la suegra	mother-in-law
el cuñado	brother-in-law
la cuñada	sister-in-law
el yerno	son-in-law
la nuera	daughter-in-law

Activity A

Match the Spanish word with its English equivalent.

> tía   nieto   prima   sobrino   abuelos   abuelo

1 cousin (f) _____

2 nephew _____

3 aunt _____

4 grandson _____

5 grandfather _____

6 grandparents _____

Activity B

How are you related? Complete the statements by circling the correct relative.

1 La hermana de mi mamá es mi…

    a tía   **b sobrina**

2 El hijo de mi tía es mi…

    a primo   **b prima**

3 La madre de mi padre es mi…

    a abuelo   **b abuela**

4 El primo de mi hijo es mi…

    a sobrino   **b nieto**

5 El padre de mi padre es mi…

    a abuelo   **b madre**

6 La sobrina de mi padre es mi…

    a primo   **b prima**

SMART TIP

Just add the suffix *–astro* or *–astra* to the names of step-family members: *hermanastro, hermanastra, hijastro, hijastra, padrastro, madrastra* (step-brother, step-sister, step-son, etc.).

Smart Phrases

Te amo.

Core Phrases

¿Tiene parientes?	Do you have any relatives?
¿Es unida su familia?	Is your family close?
Tengo una familia unida.	My family is close.
¿Eres casado/casada?	Are you married?
Soy soltero/soltera.	I'm single.
Quiero a mi familia.	I love my family.
Te quiero/amo.	I love you. (family, friends/ partner)

Activity A

Draw a line to match the questions and statements with the correct response.

1 ¿Es muy unida su familia?

2 ¡Su hermano es muy guapo! ¿Es casado?

3 ¿Tiene parientes?

4 ¿Es usted soltera?

No, soy casada. Ese es mi esposo.

Sí, mi familia es muy unida.

No, es soltero.

Sí, tengo una familia muy grande.

Activity B

What do you say if you want to...

1 ...tell your husband/wife that you love him/her?

_____

2 ...tell your mother that you love her?

_____

3 ...tell someone that your family is close?

_____

4 ...ask someone if he/she is married?

_____

Your Turn

Now talk about you and your relatives. Are you single or married? Who is married in your family? Who is single?

LESSON 8

Smart Grammar

Indefinite Articles

There are four indefinite articles in Spanish. Each article agrees with its noun in gender and number.

un	a/an	(m, sing.)
una	a/an	(f, sing.)
unos	some	(m, pl.)
unas	some	(f, pl.)

Activity A

Write the correct indefinite article and noun next to each picture.

1 _____

2 _____

3 _____

4 _____

The verb *tener* (to have)

The verb *tener* is irregular. Look at the chart for its conjugation in the present tense.

yo	tengo	I have
tú	tienes	you have
usted	tiene	you have
él/ella	tiene	he/she has
nosotros/nosotras	tenemos	we have
ustedes	tienen	you have
ellos/ellas	tienen	they have

Examples

Él tiene una prima. He has a cousin.
Nosotros tenemos un tío. We have an uncle.

Activity B

Write a sentence using the correct form of *tener*.

1 tú, hermano _____

2 yo, primo _____

3 ellos, tías _____

4 ustedes, sobrinas _____

Your Turn

Answer the following questions about your family.

1 ¿Tiene tíos? _____

2 ¿Tiene sobrinos? _____

3 ¿Tienen hijos sus tíos? _____

4 ¿Tienen hijos sus primos? _____

SMART TIP

The verb *tener* is sometimes used as the equivalent of the verb "to be." If you want to say "I'm hungry," you would say *Tengo hambre*, which literally means "I have hunger." "I'm thirsty" is *Tengo sed*, and "I'm cold" is *Tengo frío*.

Activity A

The Valdez family is having a *fiesta* (party) for Abuelo Alfonso. Gisela has brought her new boyfriend Carlos and is pointing out family members to him. Complete Gisela and Carlos's conversation about her family.

Gisela Este es mi _____, Alfonso. Y
grandfather

esta es mi _____, Ramona.
grandmother

Carlos ¿Quién es esta mujer?

Gisela Ella es mi _____, Pía y este es
cousin

su _____, Pepe.
brother

Carlos ¿Es esta tu _____?
mother

Gisela No, esa es mi _____, Consuelo.
aunt

Pía y Pepe son sus _____.
children

Carlos ¿Es esta tu madre?

Gisela No, esta es mi _____ Linda,
aunt

_____ de mi _____ José.
the wife   uncle

Él es _____ de mi _____.
the brother   father

Carlos Tu _____ es grande. Y, ¿dónde está
family

tu madre?

Gisela Mis _____ no están en la fiesta.
parents

Activity B

Tell how each person is related to Gisela. Use the correct possessive adjective before the person's title.

Example Alfonso es su abuelo.

1 Ramona _____

2 Pía y Pepe _____

3 Consuelo y Linda _____

4 José _____

Activity C

At the party, José asks Carlos questions about his family. Fill in the dialogue with Carlos's responses.

José ¿Es su familia grande o pequeña?

Carlos _____

José ¿Tiene hermanos?

Carlos _____

José ¿Tiene tíos?

Carlos _____

Activity D

Now Carlos is asking Alfonso about his family. Fill in the blanks with the correct demonstrative pronouns.

Carlos ¿Es _____ su nieto?
that

Alfonso No, _____ es mi nieto.
this

Carlos ¿Quién es _____?
that (f)

Alfonso _____ es mi sobrina.
That

Carlos ¡ _____ son sus hijas!
Those

Alfonso No, _____ son mis primas.
those

Activity E

Write a sentence telling how many children each family has.

1

_____

2

_____

3

_____

4

_____

Internet Activity

Go to **www.berlitzbooks.com/5minute** for a list of sites in Spanish where you can create a family tree. Create a family tree and label all your relatives in Spanish. Practice introducing your relatives aloud.

Unit 5 Meals

In this unit you will:
- discuss *el desayuno* (breakfast), *el almuerzo* (lunch) and *la cena* (dinner).
- use food and drink vocabulary.
- form questions in Spanish.
- use the irregular verb *querer* (to want).

LESSON 1

¡Tengo hambre!

Dialogue

Natalia and José talk about what they want to eat. Listen as they discuss food for *el desayuno*, *el almuerzo* and *la cena*. Note that as friends, Natalia and José address each other informally.

Natalia Tengo hambre. ¿Vamos a desayunar?

José Sí. Tengo ganas de ensalada.

Natalia ¿A las ocho de la mañana? La ensalada es comida de almuerzo y de cena.

José Está bien. ¿Qué quieres comer?

Natalia Huevos. ¿Quieres comer huevos?

José Sí. Pero, tengo ganas de beber vino.

Natalia ¡El vino no es para el desayuno!

Activity A

Circle **T** for true and **F** for false.

1 Natalia wants to eat breakfast.   **T/F**
2 José wants to eat salad for breakfast.   **T/F**
3 Natalia tells José that they should eat soup.   **T/F**
4 José is in the mood for a beer.   **T/F**

Activity B

Circle the correct answer.

1 What does Natalia want to eat?   **a**   **b**

2 What is José in the mood to drink?   **a**   **b**

3 What are they going to eat for breakfast?   **a**   **b**

4 What time does the dialogue take place?   **a**  **b**

> ### SMART TIP
>
> The preposition *de* has several meanings, including:
> - of (belonging)
> - of (made of)
> - from
> - for
> - to (noun + infinitive)
>
> When a nouns functions like an adjectives, use *de*. For example, the expression "It's a breakfast food" becomes *Es una comida de desayuno*.

Words to Know

Core Words

La comida (Food)

la fruta	fruit
el pan	bread
la sopa	soup

Las bebidas (Drinks)

el agua	water
el café	coffee
la cerveza	beer
el jugo	juice
la leche	milk
el té	tea

Food Verbs

beber	to drink
comer	to eat
tomar	to take/eat/drink

CULTURE TIPS

- *Sándwich* is an English word popularized in Latin America. Although *sándwich* now appears in Spanish dictionaries, *emparedado*, the original word for "sandwich," is still preferred in countries such as Spain.

- *¿Quieres ir a tomar cerveza?* (Do you want to get a beer?) In Spain you can say *Vamos por unas cañitas* (little sugar canes). In Mexico you can say *Vamos por unas chelas* (*Chela* is the diminutive for the name *Graciela*).

Activity A

Look at the pictures and write, in Spanish, the food or drink that each person enjoys.

1 _____ 2 _____

3 _____ 4 _____

Activity B

Use the word box below to tell what you eat and drink for breakfast, lunch and dinner. Be sure to use the conjunction *y* (and).

fruta	pan	cerveza	sopa	agua	café

1 desayuno _____

2 almuerzo _____

3 cena _____

SMART TIP

Think of *tomar* as the Spanish equivalent of "to have" in regards to food and drink. If you want to say that you can't have coffee, say *No puedo tomar café.*

Smart Phrases

Core Phrases

Tengo ganas de beber __.	I'm in the mood to drink __.
Tengo ganas de comer __.	I'm in the mood to eat __.
Tengo hambre.	I'm hungry.
Tengo sed.	I'm thirsty.
Vamos a almorzar.	Let's have lunch.
Vamos a cenar.	Let's have dinner.
Vamos a desayunar.	Let's have breakfast.

SMART TIP

The nouns *desayuno, almuerzo* and *cena* can be made into verbs by adding the ending *–ar*. This means that *desayuno* is the meal while *desayunar* is the action.

Activity A

Six people want different things to eat or drink. Read the items on the left and decide if the person is hungry or thirsty. Check the appropriate answer.

	Tengo hambre.	**Tengo sed.**
1 pan y fruta	☐	☐
2 leche y té	☐	☐
3 sopa y ensalada	☐	☐
4 cerveza y agua	☐	☐
5 huevos	☐	☐
6 jugo	☐	☐

Activity B

Fill in the blanks with the correct Spanish phrase.

1 _____ una ensalada.
   I'm in the mood to eat

2 _____ jugo.
   I'm in the mood to drink

Activity C

Write the correct Spanish phrase.

1 Let's have breakfast.

2 Let's have lunch.

3 Let's have dinner.

LESSON 4

Smart Grammar

Question Words

¿Cómo?	How?
¿Cuál?	Which one?
¿Cuáles?	Which ones?
¿Cuándo?	When?
¿Dónde?	Where?
¿Por qué?	Why?
¿Qué?	What?
¿Quién?	Who is?
¿Quiénes?	Who are?

SMART TIPS

- Use the upside down question mark at the beginning of a question and the regular question mark at the end.

- To begin a question, follow the upside down question mark with a question word. Then use a conjugated verb.

Examples:

¿Quién es su amigo?	Who is your friend?
¿Cuándo comemos?	When do we eat?
¿Cómo es su familia?	What's your family like?
¿Por qué hace ejercicio?	Why do you exercise every day?

- A similar rule applies to exclamations. Use the upside down exclamation mark at the beginning of an exclamation and a regular exclamation mark at the end.

Examples:

¡Vamos a comer!	Let's eat!
¡Qué buena está la ensalada!	This salad is very good!

Activity A

Fill in the blanks with the correct question word. Choose the word from the word box.

Quién	Dónde	Cuál	Cuándo

1 ¿_____ vive?

2 ¿_____ es su dirección?

3 ¿_____ toma cerveza?

4 ¿_____ va al cine?

Activity B

Ask questions using the following question words.

1 ¿Cuáles _____?

2 ¿Cómo _____?

3 ¿Por qué _____?

4 ¿Qué _____?

5 ¿Quiénes _____?

Activity C

What question word do you use to ask…

1 …for a reason?

_____

2 …who someone is?

_____

3 …when an event is going to happen?

_____

4 …which object someone is pointing to?

_____

5 …where someone lives?

_____

Your Turn

Read the following answers. Then ask a question for each answer. Practice this in front of a mirror. Saying the questions and answers aloud and watching how your mouth moves will help your pronunciation.

1 Mi madre es María.

2 Son las tres de la tarde.

3 Ellos son los primos de Gustavo.

4 Este es mi primo.

En el restaurante

Menu

Read the menu aloud. Next, listen to the dialogue. Marta talks to *el mesero* (the waiter) about what she will order at the restaurant.

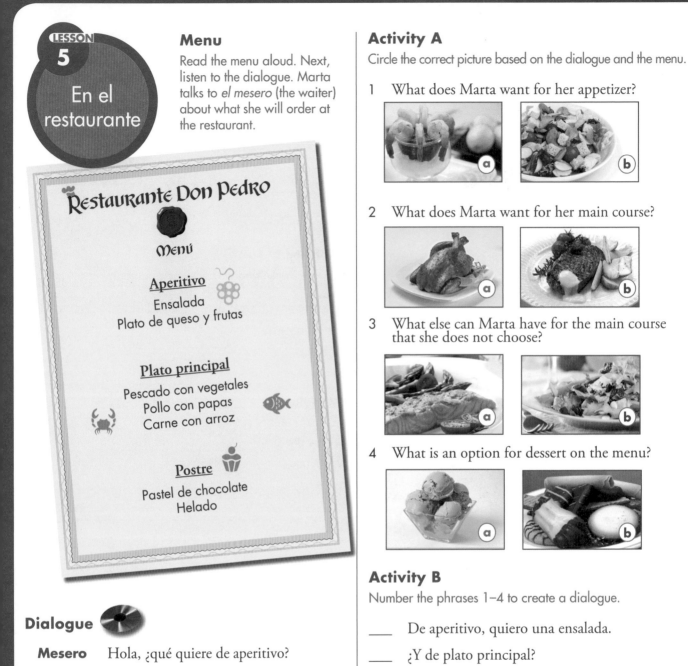

Restaurante Don Pedro

Menú

Aperitivo
Ensalada
Plato de queso y frutas

Plato principal
Pescado con vegetales
Pollo con papas
Carne con arroz

Postre
Pastel de chocolate
Helado

Dialogue

Mesero	Hola, ¿qué quiere de aperitivo?
Marta	De aperitivo, quiero una ensalada.
Mesero	Muy bien. ¿Y de plato principal?
Marta	¿Qué me recomienda?
Mesero	El pescado con vegetales. Está delicioso.
Marta	No quiero el pescado. No me gusta.
Mesero	El pollo con papas también es muy bueno.
Marta	Está bien. Quiero el pollo.
Mesero	Bien. Pronto llega su comida.

Activity A

Circle the correct picture based on the dialogue and the menu.

1 What does Marta want for her appetizer?

a   b

2 What does Marta want for her main course?

a   b

3 What else can Marta have for the main course that she does not choose?

a   b

4 What is an option for dessert on the menu?

a   b

Activity B

Number the phrases 1–4 to create a dialogue.

____ De aperitivo, quiero una ensalada.

____ ¿Y de plato principal?

____ ¿Qué quiere de aperitivo?

____ Quiero el pollo.

CULTURE TIP

Apart from saying *por favor* (please) and *gracias* (thank you), good manners in Spain and Latin America include saying *buen provecho* (enjoy your meal) before and/or after a meal.

Words to Know

Más comida (More Food)

el arroz	rice
la carne	meat
la ensalada	salad
el helado	ice cream
las papas	potatoes
el pastel	cake
el pescado	fish
el pollo	chicken
el queso	cheese
los vegetales	vegetables

Activity A

Decide whether each set of food items is an appetizer, a main course or a dessert. On the lines provided, write *aperitivo, plato principal* or *postre.*

1 la ensalada y el plato de queso _____

2 la carne y el pescado _____

3 el helado y el pastel _____

4 el pollo y la pasta _____

CULTURE TIP

While *el mesero/la mesera* is most common in Latin America, in some countries, including Spain, you use *el camarero/la camarera* to refer to your waiter.

Activity B

Use the menu on page 48 to answer the following questions in Spanish. Be sure to write complete sentences.

1 ¿Cuál es un aperitivo?

_____

2 ¿Cuál es un plato principal?

_____

3 ¿Cuál es un postre?

_____

4 ¿Qué viene con el pescado?

_____

Your Turn

Use your new vocabulary and phrases to create your own menu.

Restaurante _____

Menú

Aperitivo

_____

_____

Plato principal

_____

_____

Postre

_____

_____

Bebidas

_____

_____

LESSON 7
Smart Phrases

Core Phrases

Buen provecho.	Enjoy your meal.
¿Cómo está su comida?	How is your food?
¿Cuál es la especialidad del día?	What is today's special?
La especialidad es ___.	The special is ___.
¡Está delicioso/deliciosa!	This is delicious!
La cuenta, por favor.	The check, please.
¿Puedo ver la carta de vinos?	May I see the wine list?
Yo invito.	It's on me.

Activity A

What do you say if you want to…

1 …tell someone to enjoy his/her meal?

_____

2 …ask the waiter for the check?

_____

3 …say that something tastes delicious?

_____

4 …ask for the wine list?

_____

CULTURE TIPS

- Lunch is the heaviest meal in Spain and most Latin American countries.

- For dinner, people in Spain usually have *tapas* (small portions of different foods). In Mexico, people usually buy *antojitos* on the street. *Antojitos* are snacks, but they can be heavy. There are *tostadas, tamales, tacos, gorditas, quesadillas* and many more!

Activity B

Circle the best response to the questions and scenarios below.

1 ¿Cuál es la especialidad del día?

   a **¡Está delicioso!**

   b **La especialidad es el pescado.**

2 It is the beginning of the meal and you want something to drink. You say to *el mesero*:

   a **¿Puedo ver la carta de vinos?**

   b **Buen provecho.**

3 You are eating and the waiter wants to know if you like the food. You answer:

   a **La especialidad es la carne.**

   b **Está delicioso/deliciosa.**

4 It is the end of the meal. You say to *el mesero:*

   a **La cuenta, por favor.**

   b **¿Cuál es la especialidad del día?**

Your Turn

You are at a restaurant with a friend. Tell him about the food, the menu and the specials. Ask him about his food. At the end, be polite and take care of the check.

Smart Grammar

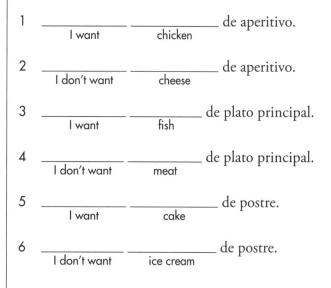

Activity B

What do you want to eat? Complete the sentences below with the *yo* form of *querer* to explain what you do and do not want to eat.

1 _____ _____ de aperitivo.
      I want   chicken

2 _____ _____ de aperitivo.
    I don't want   cheese

3 _____ _____ de plato principal.
      I want   fish

4 _____ _____ de plato principal.
    I don't want   meat

5 _____ _____ de postre.
      I want   cake

6 _____ _____ de postre.
    I don't want   ice cream

The verb *querer* (to want)

The verb *querer* is irregular. The chart shows its conjugation in the present tense.

yo	quiero	I want
tú	quieres	you want
usted	quiere	you want
él/ella	quiere	he/she wants
nosotros/nosotras	queremos	we want
ustedes	quieren	you want
ellos/ellas	quieren	they want

SMART TIPS

- When some irregular verbs such as *querer* are conjugated, the *e* before the last syllable changes to an *ie* in every person but *nosotros*. Try this rule with the verb *preferir* (to prefer).

- Add *no* before the appropriate conjugation of *querer* to indicate the negative form of the verb. For example, *No quiero postre* (I don't want dessert).

Your Turn

¿Quiere carne o vegetales? Say out loud which food items you want to eat. Then use *preferir* to say which food items you prefer.

el pescado

la ensalada

el pollo

las papas

Activity A

Write the correct form of the verb *querer* to complete the phrases.

1 Ella no _____ el pollo de plato principal.

2 Nosotros _____ el queso de aperitivo.

3 Ellos _____ helado de postre.

4 ¿ _____ Luis la carne de plato principal?

Unit 5 Review

Activity A

Look at the pictures, then write complete sentences to say what people want for lunch and what they prefer for dinner. Use the personal pronouns yo, *tú*, *él*, *nosotras*, *ustedes* and *ellos*. One sentence has been done for you.

De almuerzo (querer)

1 Quiero comer sopa y beber agua.

2 _____

3 _____

4 _____

5 _____

6 _____

De cena (preferir)

1 _____

2 _____

3 _____

4 _____

5 _____

6 Prefieren comer carne y beber cerveza.

Activity B

There has been a mix-up with the menus at el Café Español. Someone put desserts under appetizers and main dishes under desserts! Cross out the mistakes and replace them with the correct words.

CAFÉ ESPAÑOL

Menú

Aperitivo
Pastel de chocolate
Ensalada

Plato principal
Pollo con vegetales
Plato de queso y frutas

Postre
Carne con papas
Pescado

Activity C

Julio is hungry, so he and Eva go out to dinner. Use the phrases and question words you learned in this unit to fill in the blanks of their dialogue.

Julio _____ hambre.

Eva ¿_____ quieres comer?

Julio _____ de comer pollo.

Eva Vamos a _____.

In the car

Julio ¿_____ está el restaurante?

Eva Está ahí. (Points to a restaurant down the block.)

At the restaurant before eating

Eva ¿Qué _____ de plato principal?

Julio Quiero _____.

At the restaurant after eating

Eva Mesero, _____, por favor.

Challenge

Look at the word *naranja*. What do you think it means? (Hint: It's a type of fruit.) After you take a guess at its meaning, look up the word in a Spanish-English dictionary to see if you're right. Then look up other kinds of fruit to further expand your vocabulary. Repeat the activity with other food items as well. Visit **www.berlitzbooks.com/5minute** for a list of online dictionaries.

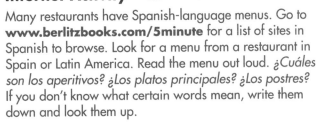

Internet Activity

Many restaurants have Spanish-language menus. Go to **www.berlitzbooks.com/5minute** for a list of sites in Spanish to browse. Look for a menu from a restaurant in Spain or Latin America. Read the menu out loud. ¿Cuáles son los aperitivos? ¿Los platos principales? ¿Los postres? If you don't know what certain words mean, write them down and look them up.

Unit 6 Weather and Temperature

In this unit, you will:
- talk about temperature, weather and seasons.
- learn the irregular verb *estar* (to be).
- learn the present progressive tense.

LESSON 1

¿Cómo está el clima?

Dialogue

Oliver lives in Mexico and Fernanda lives in Peru. Listen to their phone conversation about the weather in their countries.

Oliver Hola, Fernanda. ¿Cómo está el clima en Perú?

Fernanda Hace frío. Está soleado pero estamos a siete grados centígrados.

Oliver ¿Sí? También hace mal tiempo en México.

Fernanda ¿Cuál es la temperatura?

Oliver Treinta y cinco grados centígrados, y hay lluvia.

Fernanda ¿Treinta y cinco grados? ¡Eso es buen tiempo!

Activity A

Match the questions with the correct picture.

1 ¿Cómo está el clima en Perú? _____

2 ¿Cómo está el clima en México? _____

3 ¿Cuál es la temperatura en Perú? _____

4 ¿Cuál es la temperatura en México? _____

Activity B

Reread the dialogue and look for words to complete the crossword below. Three out of the six words are cognates (words that are similar in Spanish and English).

ACROSS
5 temperature
6 cold

DOWN
1 centigrade
2 weather
3 sunny
4 degrees

SMART TIP

The word *también* means "also" and "too." For example:
También hace frío en México. It's also cold in México.
Yo también tengo frío. I'm cold too.

In most Spanish-speaking countries, *la temperatura* (temperature) is measured in *grados Celsius* or *grados centígrados* (Celsius or centigrade). The most common term is *grados centígrados*.

To convert Fahrenheit to Celsius, use this formula:

$C = (F - 32) \div 1.8$

And Celsius to Fahrenheit:

$F = (1.8 \times C) + 32$

Core Words

cálido	warm
calor	hot
el clima	weather
con viento	windy
frío	cold
húmedo	humid
lluvioso	rainy
nublado	cloudy
soleado	sunny

Activity A

Use the vocabulary to complete the dialogue.

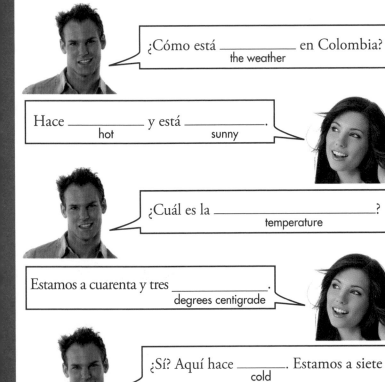

¿Cómo está _____ en Colombia?
(the weather)

Hace _____ y está _____.
(hot)   (sunny)

¿Cuál es la _____?
(temperature)

Estamos a cuarenta y tres _____.
(degrees centigrade)

¿Sí? Aquí hace _____. Estamos a siete
(cold)

grados _____.
(centigrade)

Activity B

Circle the appropriate word or phrase to complete each thought.

1 It's a nice day.

   a Estamos a veinticinco   **b Hace frío.**
     grados centígrados.

2 It's 2 degrees Celsius.

   a Hace calor.   **b Hace frío.**

3 It's raining and it's windy. This describes:

   a la temperatura   **b el clima**

4 It's 6 degrees Celsius outside. This is:

   a el clima   **b la temperatura**

Activity C

Match the appropriate word to each picture.

1 nublado   **a**

2 lluvioso   **b**

3 con viento   **c**

4 soleado   **d**

Smart Phrases

Core Phrases

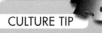

¿Cuál es la temperatura?	What's the temperature?
Estamos a ___ grados centígrados.	It's ___ degrees Celsius.
¿Cómo está el clima?	What's the weather like?
Hace calor/frío.	It's hot/cold.
Está soleado.	It's sunny.
Hace mal/buen tiempo.	The weather is bad/nice.

Extra Phrases

Está lloviendo.	It's raining.
Está nevando.	It's snowing.

CULTURE TIP

If someone is talking about the weather and you hear *Llueve a cántaros,* you better bring your *paraguas* (umbrella). Literally meaning "It's raining buckets," it is the equivalent to the English expression "It's raining cats and dogs."

Activity A

Write each word or phrase in the appropriate column.

> 35°C   Hace calor.   6°C
> Hace buen tiempo.   32°F   Hace frío.

¿Cuál es la temperatura?   ¿Cómo está el clima?

_____   _____

_____   _____

_____   _____

Activity B

¿Cómo está el clima? Match each picture with the best description of the weather.

1    **a** Hace calor.

2   **b** Está soleado.

3    **c** Hace mal tiempo.

4   **d** Hace frío.

Activity C

Imagine it is a warm spring day. Read the questions and circle the appropriate answers.

1 ¿Cómo está el clima?

   a Hace buen tiempo.   **b** Hace mal tiempo.

2 ¿Hace calor o frío?

   a Hace calor.   **b** Hace frío.

3 ¿Cuál es la temperatura?

   a Estamos a cinco grados centígrados.   **b** Estamos a veintiséis grados centígrados.

The verb *estar* (to be)

In Spanish, there are two forms of the verb "to be." You learned *ser* in Unit 1. Now you will learn several uses for *estar*.

Estar is usually used to describe a state of being that is not permanent: *Estoy cansado* (I am tired). You are not permanently tired but tired at the moment.

Estar is also used to talk about location. If you want to ask where something is, you say *¿Dónde está?* (Where is it?) The response could be *Está aquí* (It's here).

yo	estoy	I am
tú	estás	you are
usted	está	you are
él/ella	está	he/she is
nosotros/nosotras	estamos	we are
ustedes	están	you are
ellos/ellas	están	they are

Activity A

Fill in the blanks with the correct form of *estar*.

1 _____ nublado.

2 _____ lluvioso.

3 Tú _____ alegre (happy).

4 Yo _____ triste (sad).

5 ¿Dónde _____ María?

6 ¿Dónde _____ José Luis y Lupita?

7 Mi hermana y yo _____ en Barcelona.

8 Mis padres _____ en Acapulco.

Activity B

Write the correct form of *estar* in the blanks below.

1   El día _____ soleado.

2   El día _____ frío.

3 _____ a cinco grados.

4 _____ nublado.

Your Turn

Now talk about you, the place you are at and the weather in that place. *¿Cómo está? ¿Está triste o alegre? ¿Dónde está? ¿Cómo está el clima?*

LESSON 5

¿Qué está haciendo?

What are you doing? Read this fact sheet and *la entrevista* (interview) with Antonio Blanco, a famous soccer player. Take a look to see what Antonio likes to do and wear for each season.

Nombre Antonio Blanco
Edad 33 años
Nacionalidad Argentina
Ocupación Jugador de fútbol
Actividades preferidas
correr   jugar fútbol   viajar   nadar

Entrevista

Reportera ¿Qué hace usualmente durante el verano?

Antonio En el verano juego fútbol, nado y corro.

Reportera ¿No viaja durante el verano?

Antonio No, viajar durante el verano es aburrido. En el verano estoy en México. En el invierno viajo un poco por Europa.

Reportera En el verano no necesita mucha ropa: sandalias, pantalones cortos y ya está. Pero en el invierno…

Antonio Tiene razón. En el invierno hace frío en Europa. Uso una chaqueta, una bufanda, guantes y botas.

Reportera Tengo esta foto de usted. ¿Dónde está en esta foto?

Antonio Estoy en Lima, Perú.

Activity A

Complete the word web with the activities Antonio does in the summer.

actividades en el verano

Complete the word web with the clothing Antonio wears in the winter.

ropa de invierno

Activity B

Complete the following sentences about Antonio.

1 Antonio swims, runs and _____ in the summer.

2 Antonio travels in the _____.

3 Antonio wears a jacket in the _____.

4 Antonio is from _____ and is _____ years old.

CULTURE TIP

While *fútbol* is the Spanish term for soccer, don't confuse it with *fútbol americano* (American football).

Smart Phrases

Core Phrases

¿Qué hace usualmente?	What do you usually do?
¿Qué está haciendo?	What are you doing?
Es aburrido.	It's boring.
Es divertido.	It's fun.
Tiene razón.	You're right.
Durante el verano yo usualmente ___.	In the summer, I usually ___.

Activity A

¿Qué piensa? (What do you think?) Write *es aburrido* or *es divertido* to indicate what you think about each activity.

1

_____

2

_____

3

_____

4

_____

Activity B

What do you say if you want to…

1   …ask someone what he or she is doing?

_____

2   …ask someone what he or she usually does?

_____

3   …tell what you usually do *durante el invierno*?

_____

4   …tell someone he or she is right?

_____

Your Turn

Complete the phrases with your favorite or not so favorite activities.

1   _____ es divertido.

2   _____ es aburrido.

3   _____ es divertido.

4   _____ es aburrido.

> **SMART PRONUNCIATION**
>
> In Latin American Spanish, the *z* is pronounced like the *s* in "same." So *razón* is pronounced rah•sohn. In Spain, however, the *z* is pronounced like the *th* in "thin." So *razón* is also pronounced rah•thon.

Words to Know

Core Words

La ropa (Clothing)

las botas	boots
la chaqueta	jacket
los guantes	gloves
las sandalias	sandals
el sombrero	hat

Las estaciones (Seasons)

el invierno	winter
el otoño	autumn
la primavera	spring
el verano	summer

Extra Words

nadar	to swim
usar	to wear, to use
viajar	to travel

Activity A
Write the Spanish word for each image.

1
_____

2
_____

3
_____

4
_____

Activity B
Use the words in the box to name the season in each picture.

> el invierno   la primavera   el verano   el otoño

1
_____

2
_____

3
_____

4
_____

Activity C
Write the Spanish word or words to complete each sentence.

1 Uso _____ en el otoño.
        a hat

2 Tú usas _____ en el invierno.
         gloves

3 Ella usa una _____ en la primavera.
              jacket

4 Mi abuela usa _____ en el verano.
               sandals

The verb *jugar* (to play)

The verb *jugar* is irregular. The chart shows its conjugation in the present tense.

yo	juego	I play
tú	juegas	you play
usted	juega	you play
él/ella	juega	he/she plays
nosotros/nosotras	jugamos	we play
ustedes	juegan	you play
ellos/ellas	juegan	they play

Activity A

Write sentences in Spanish saying who plays *fútbol*.

1 (María) _____

2 (nosotros) _____

3 (yo) _____

4 (ellas) _____

Activity B

A qué juega? (What do you play?) Use the correct form of *jugar* to answer the question.

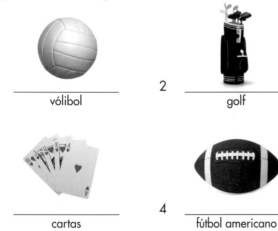

1 _____
vólibol

2 _____
golf

3 _____
cartas

4 _____
fútbol americano

The Present Progressive

The present progressive tense indicates an action that is currently taking place.

Verbs that End in *–ar*

estar (conjugated) + verb stem + *–ando*
Example *jugar* ⟶ *jugando*
Ella está jugando.   She is playing.

Verbs that End in *–er* and *–ir*

estar (conjugated) + verb stem + *–iendo*
Example *correr* ⟶ *corriendo*
Estamos corriendo.   We are running.
Example *subir* (to go up) ⟶ *subiendo*
Ustedes están subiendo   You are walking up
   las escaleras.   the stairs.

Activity C

Write the present progressive form of each verb.

1 viajar ⟶ _____

2 jugar ⟶ _____

3 hacer ⟶ _____

4 nadar ⟶ _____

Activity D

Look at each picture and write what is happening.

1 yo: viajar

_____

2 él: jugar

_____

3 ellos: correr

_____

4 tú: nadar

_____

Activity A

As you know, *estar* is very similar to *ser*, yet it has different uses. Circle the verb you would use to say these phrases in Spanish.

1   I am studying.   **ser**   **estar**

2   I am Spanish.   **ser**   **estar**

3   She is from Peru.   **ser**   **estar**

4   We are bored.   **ser**   **estar**

5   It is raining.   **ser**   **estar**

Activity B

Now write the phrases in Spanish.

1   _____

2   _____

3   _____

4   _____

5   _____

Activity C

Complete the word search to find words related to the weather and seasons.

sol	cálido	temperatura	soleado	estar
llevar	chaqueta	primavera	jugar	

```
B P E V Z L Z S C S H K W Y J
X C L A C H A Q U E T A W V V
Q P Y C X Q Z M K D Y D P Y C
F D S L A P R I M A V E R A E
X D O B M N A B R Z E K P E S
Q Á L F L M S O L E A D O I T
F Q E A T E M P E R A T U R A
P Z Z Z Q G A L Q A W P E H R
Y E S T Á C Á L I D O D L L F
A I J U G A R E G Q J T J K W
B K V F Z R H V R E P J U O D
S Q W R J P K A P P J R N Y U
I T Y T A E Á R D B X L Q X N
```

Activity D

¿Qué está pensando Estela? (What is Estela thinking?) Estela is going out, but before leaving she sees that it's raining. Use the correct form of each verb to complete Estela's thoughts as she gets ready to go out.

> Está _____.
>   llover
> ¿Dónde está mi paraguas?
>
> Aquí está.

> También _____ frío.
>   hacer
> ¿Dónde _____ mi chaqueta?
>   estar
> Aquí está.

> Mmmm, _____ mucho.
>   llover
> ¿Dónde están mis botas?
>
> ¡Es tarde!

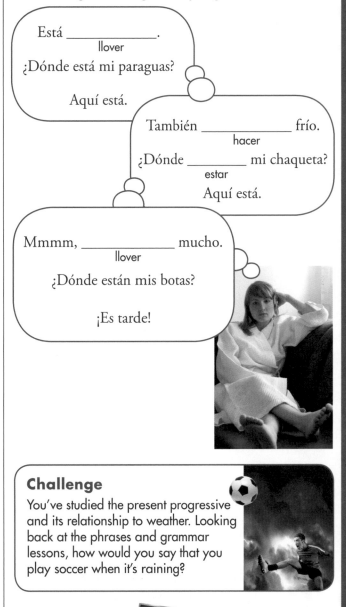

Challenge

You've studied the present progressive and its relationship to weather. Looking back at the phrases and grammar lessons, how would you say that you play soccer when it's raining?

Internet Activity

Wonder what the weather is like in other countries? Go to **www.berlitzbooks.com/5minute** for a list of weather sites in Spanish. Find out what's happening in Tijuana right now. What about Veracruz and Los Cabos? Describe what you find in Spanish.

Unit 7 Shopping

In this unit you will:
- use vocabulary related to shopping and payment.
- ask for pieces of clothing and sizes.
- make comparisons with "more than" and "less than."
- learn reflexive verbs such as *probarse* (to try on) and *vestirse* (to put on).
- use indefinite pronouns such as *alguien* (someone) and *alguno* (some).

LESSON 1

La tienda de ropa

Dialogue

Anita is at *una tienda de ropa* (a clothing store). She is looking for a dress. Listen as she talks to *el vendedor* (shop assistant).

Vendedor Buenos días. ¿En qué la puedo ayudar?

Anita Estoy buscando un vestido.

Vendedor Aquí están los vestidos. ¿Qué talla necesita?

Anita Talla mediana por favor.

Vendedor Bien. ¿De qué color quiere el vestido?

Anita Quiero un vestido azul.

Vendedor Aquí está. ¿Quiere probarse el vestido?

Anita Sí. Me lo pruebo.

Activity A

Circle the correct picture.

1 Which item is Anita looking for?

   a   b   c

2 What size does Anita want?

   a   b   c

3 What color does Anita want?

   a   b   c

Activity B

Match the Spanish questions with their English translations.

1 ¿En qué la puedo ayudar?
   a How can I help you?
   b How would you like to pay?

2 ¿Qué talla necesita?
   a What color would you like?
   b What size do you need?

3 ¿De qué color quiere el vestido?
   a What color dress would you like?
   b What size dress do you want?

LESSON 2

Smart Phrases

Core Phrases

Estoy buscando _____.	I'm looking for _____.
Quiero comprar un/una ___.	I want to buy a _____.
¿Qué talla necesita?	What size do you need?
Necesito la talla _____.	I need a size _____.
El vestido es grande/pequeño.	The dress is large/small.
La camisa me queda apretada/floja.	The shirt is tight/loose on me.
¿En qué lo/la puedo ayudar?	How can I help you (m/f)?
¿Algo más?	Anything else?
¿Quiere probarse _____?	Do you want to try __ on?
Me lo/la pruebo.	I'll try it on.

Activity A

Choose the best response.

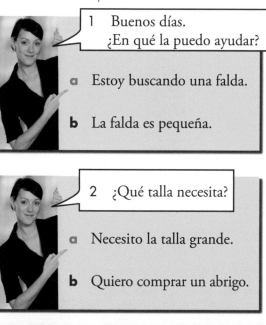

1 Buenos días.
¿En qué la puedo ayudar?

   a Estoy buscando una falda.

   b La falda es pequeña.

2 ¿Qué talla necesita?

   a Necesito la talla grande.

   b Quiero comprar un abrigo.

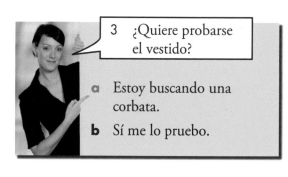

3 ¿Quiere probarse el vestido?

   a Estoy buscando una corbata.

   b Sí me lo pruebo.

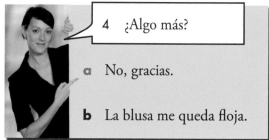

4 ¿Algo más?

   a No, gracias.

   b La blusa me queda floja.

Activity B

Respond with one of the phrases you've learned.

1 ¿En qué lo puedo ayudar?

_____.
Say that you are looking for a dress.

2 ¿Algo más?

_____.
Say that you need a medium shirt.

3 ¿Algo más?

_____.
Say that you want to buy a skirt.

4 ¿Qué talla necesita?

_____.
Say that you wear a small.

SMART TIP

The word *algo* is very versatile. In Spanish, *algo* is the English equivalent of both "anything" and "something." So, if someone asks you ¿*Algo más?* (Anything else?) you can respond *Sí, quiero algo más* (Yes, I'd like something else).

Words to Know

Core Phrases

La ropa (Clothing)

el abrigo	coat
la blusa	blouse
la camisa	shirt
la camiseta	T-shirt
la corbata	tie
la falda	skirt
los pantalones	pants
el vestido	dress

Las tallas (Sizes)

pequeña	small
mediana	medium
grande	large
extra grande	extra large

Los colores (Colors)

amarillo	yellow
azul	blue
morado	purple
negro	black
rojo	red
rosa	pink
verde	green

CULTURE TIP

Various words are used for "jeans," depending on the country, or even region, you are in. *Vaqueros* (literally, cowboys) and *tejanos* are mostly used in Spain. Though *vaqueros* is understood and sometimes used in other Spanish-speaking countries, other terms are more common. *Pantalones de mezclilla* is used in Mexico, *pitusa* in Cuba and *mahones* in the Dominican Republic and Puerto Rico. Use of the English word "jeans" itself, sometimes pronounced *yeens*, is becoming more frequent in many Spanish-speaking countries.

Activity A

Label the clothing in Spanish.

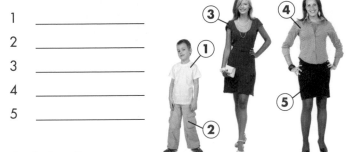

1 _____

2 _____

3 _____

4 _____

5 _____

Activity B

Read each sentence, then circle the item you are looking for.

1 Estoy buscando una blusa rosa.

    a   b

2 Estoy buscando una corbata roja.

    a   b

3 Estoy buscando una camiseta extra grande.

    a   XL   b   M

4 Estoy buscando un abrigo negro.

    a   b

SMART TIP

In some Spanish-speaking countries the English abbreviations S, M, L and XL are used to mark the clothing sizes *pequeña, mediana, grande* and *extra grande*. In other countries you will probably see *P, M, G* and *EG.*

Smart Grammar

Reflexive Verbs

- *Vestirse* (to get dressed, literally: to dress oneself) and *probarse* (to try on) are reflexive verbs. Reflexive verbs are for actions a person does to, at or for himself or herself.

- To conjugate a reflexive verb, drop the *–se* ending, follow the regular conjugation pattern and use a reflexive pronoun before the verb (see below).

Reflexive Pronouns

yo	me	myself
tú	te	yourself
usted	se	yourself
él/ella	se	himself/herself
nosotros/nosotras	nos	ourselves
ustedes	se	yourselves
ellos/ellas	se	themselves

Vestirse (to get dressed)

yo	me visto	I get dressed
tú	te vistes	you get dressed
usted	se viste	you get dressed
él/ella	se viste	he/she gets dressed
nosotros/nosotras	nos vestimos	we get dressed
ustedes	se visten	you get dressed
ellos/ellas	se visten	they get dressed

Activity A

Fill in the blanks with the correct reflexive pronoun.

1 Él _____ viste a las ocho.

2 Nosotros _____ probamos los abrigos.

3 Ellas _____ visten en la mañana.

4 Tú _____ pruebas una falda.

Activity B

Write the correct conjugation of the verb *vestirse* to complete each sentence.

1 Ustedes se _____ en la tarde.

2 Te _____ a las nueve.

3 Yo me _____ en la mañana.

4 Nos _____ para la fiesta.

5 Mis padres se _____ en su recámara.

SMART TIPS

- When there are two verbs, you can place the reflexive pronoun before the conjugated verb or after the infinitive. For example: *Me quiero vestir* or *Quiero vestirme* (I want to get dressed).

- Another common reflexive verb is *probarse* (to try on). Like *vestirse*, the conjugations change more than the ending of the verb. Except in the *nosotros/nosotras* form, the o changes to ue. If you want to say "I try on a shirt," you would say *Me pruebo una camisa*.

Your Turn

Complete the conjugation chart for *probarse*. Some are done for you. If you're not sure, look at the answer key in the back of the book.

yo	me	
tú	te	pruebas
usted	se	
él/ella	se	
nosotros/nosotras	nos	probamos
ustedes	se	
ellos/ellas	se	

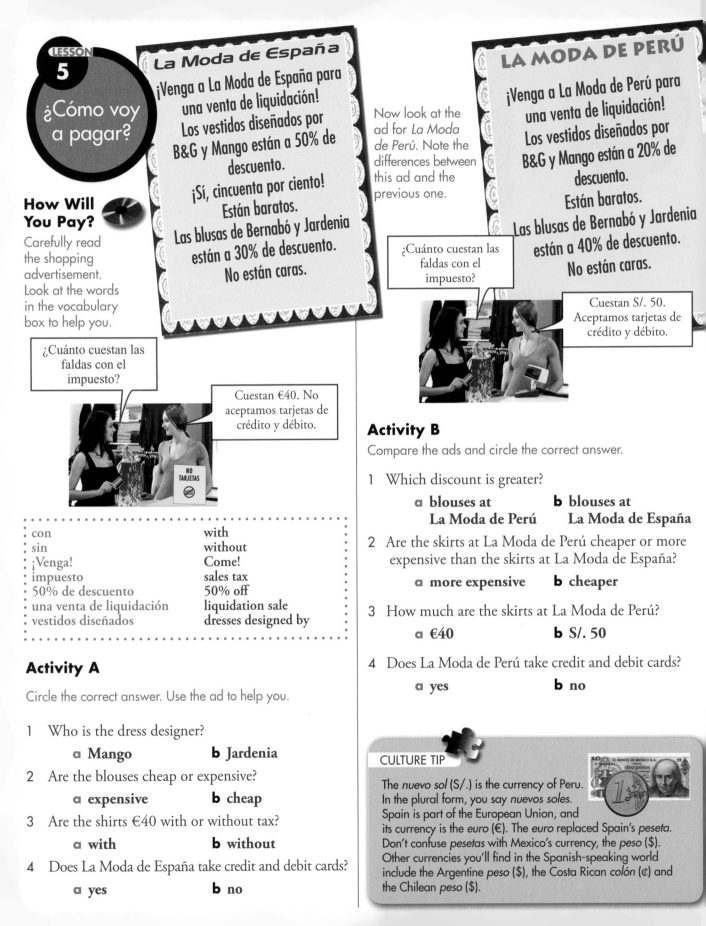

LESSON 5

¿Cómo voy a pagar?

How Will You Pay?

Carefully read the shopping advertisement. Look at the words in the vocabulary box to help you.

La Moda de España

¡Venga a La Moda de España para una venta de liquidación!

Los vestidos diseñados por B&G y Mango están a 50% de descuento.

¡Sí, cincuenta por ciento!

Están baratos.

Las blusas de Bernabó y Jardenia están a 30% de descuento.

No están caras.

¿Cuánto cuestan las faldas con el impuesto?

Cuestan €40. No aceptamos tarjetas de crédito y débito.

NO TARJETAS

---

con	with
sin	without
¡Venga!	Come!
impuesto	sales tax
50% de descuento	50% off
una venta de liquidación	liquidation sale
vestidos diseñados	dresses designed by

Activity A

Circle the correct answer. Use the ad to help you.

1 Who is the dress designer?

   a Mango   **b** Jardenia

2 Are the blouses cheap or expensive?

   a expensive   **b** cheap

3 Are the shirts €40 with or without tax?

   a with   **b** without

4 Does La Moda de España take credit and debit cards?

   a yes   **b** no

Now look at the ad for *La Moda de Perú*. Note the differences between this ad and the previous one.

LA MODA DE PERÚ

¡Venga a La Moda de Perú para una venta de liquidación!

Los vestidos diseñados por B&G y Mango están a 20% de descuento.

Están baratos.

Las blusas de Bernabó y Jardenia están a 40% de descuento.

No están caras.

¿Cuánto cuestan las faldas con el impuesto?

Cuestan S/. 50. Aceptamos tarjetas de crédito y débito.

Activity B

Compare the ads and circle the correct answer.

1 Which discount is greater?

   a blouses at La Moda de Perú   **b** blouses at La Moda de España

2 Are the skirts at La Moda de Perú cheaper or more expensive than the skirts at La Moda de España?

   a more expensive   **b** cheaper

3 How much are the skirts at La Moda de Perú?

   a €40   **b** S/. 50

4 Does La Moda de Perú take credit and debit cards?

   a yes   **b** no

CULTURE TIP

The *nuevo sol* (S/.) is the currency of Peru. In the plural form, you say *nuevos soles*. Spain is part of the European Union, and its currency is the *euro* (€). The *euro* replaced Spain's *peseta*. Don't confuse *pesetas* with Mexico's currency, the *peso* ($). Other currencies you'll find in the Spanish-speaking world include the Argentine *peso* ($), the Costa Rican *colón* (₡) and the Chilean *peso* ($).

Core Phrases

¿Acepta tarjetas de crédito y débito/cheques?	Do you accept credit and debit cards/checks?
Sí, aceptamos ___.	Yes, we accept ___.
¿Cuánto cuesta la falda?	How much is the skirt?
¿Cuánto cuestan los pantalones?	How much are the pants?
¡Están baratas!	They're cheap!
¡(No) es (muy) caro!	That's (not/too) expensive!
Voy a pagar con tarjeta de crédito.	I'll pay by credit card.

Extra Phrases

Aquí está el cambio/el recibo.	Here's your change/receipt.
Quiero comprarlo/comprarla.	I want to buy it. (m/f)
Quiero comprarlos/comprarlas.	I want to buy them. (m/f)
Sólo estoy mirando.	I'm just looking.

Activity A

What do you say when you want to…

1   …ask if the shop accepts debit cards?

_____

2   …ask how much a skirt is?

_____

3   …ask if the shop accepts checks?

_____

4   …say you'll pay by credit card?

_____

5   …ask how much pants are?

_____

Activity B

Look at each picture and choose the word that best completes each statement.

> caros   barata   muy cara   baratos

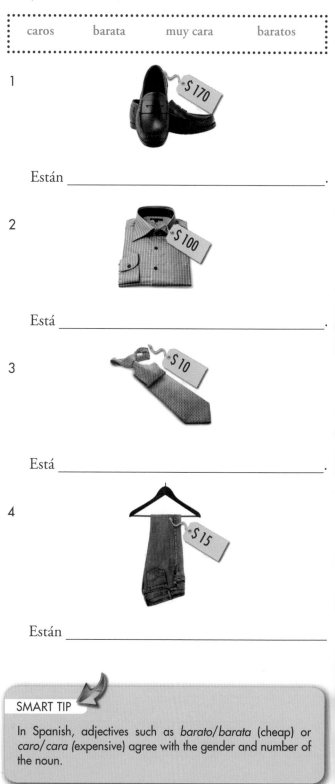

1

Están _____.

2

Está _____.

3

Está _____.

4

Están _____.

> **SMART TIP**
>
> In Spanish, adjectives such as *barato/barata* (cheap) or *caro/cara* (expensive) agree with the gender and number of the noun.

LESSON 7

Words to Know

Core Words

el cheque	check
el dinero	money
el dólar	dollar
el efectivo	cash
el impuesto	tax
el recibo	receipt
la tarjeta de crédito	credit card
la tarjeta de débito	debit card

Extra Words

la billetera	wallet
el cambio	change
los centavos	cents
la moneda	coin

Activity A

Complete the sentences with the appropriate Spanish word.

1 ¿Acepta un _____?
   <u>check</u>

Activity B

Fill in the blanks with the correct Spanish words to complete Jaime's thought bubble. Use the English translations as clues.

Tengo 500 _____ en _____
            dollars   cash
en mi billetera. También tengo una

_____. Voy a comprar mucha
credit card

ropa porque no hay _____.
                       tax

SMART TIP

If you want to say you'll pay with something, use the Spanish conjunction *con*.

Voy a pagar con tarjeta de crédito.   I'll pay with a credit card.

There is an exception for cash. You would use the preposition *en*: *Voy a pagar en efectivo.*

2 Voy a pagar con _____.
                      debit card

3 Aquí esta _____.
              the receipt

4 No tengo _____.
              money

Más que (More Than) and *menos que* (Less Than)

The phrases *más que* and *menos que* are used to make comparisons. The phrases are used in the same way as their English equivalents, for example:

Tengo más dinero que Julio.	I have more money than Julio.
Julio tiene menos dinero que yo.	Julio has less money than I do.
El abrigo cuesta más que la corbata.	The coat costs more than the tie.
La corbata cuesta menos que el abrigo.	The tie costs less than the coat.

Activity A

Look at the items in the store, then decide which cost more and which cost less. Write *más que* or *menos que* in the blanks to complete the phrases.

1   El vestido cuesta _____ la camisa.

2   Los pantalones cuestan _____ el abrigo.

3   El abrigo cuesta _____ el vestido.

4   La camisa cuesta _____ los pantalones.

Indefinite Pronouns

Indefinite pronouns are used when talking about an unspecified noun. For example, in Lesson 2 we used the indefinite pronoun *algo*, which means something or anything. There are many other indefinite pronouns in Spanish. Here are a few:

> **alguien**
> someone, somebody, anyone or anybody
>
> **Example** Conozco a alguien que vive en Canadá.
> I know someone who lives in Canada.
>
> **alguno, alguna, algunos, algunas**
> one or some (people or things)
>
> **Example** Necesito algunas monedas.
> I need some coins.
>
> **ninguno, ninguna**
> no one, nobody, none
>
> **Example** Ninguno de ellos come carne.
> None of them eats meat.
>
> **nadie**
> no one, nobody
>
> **Example** Nadie vive ahí.
> No one lives there.

Activity B

Circle the correct indefinite pronoun for each sentence.

1   **¿Alguno   Alguien**   quiere comer?

2   **Ninguna   Nadie**   de ellas estudia español.

3   **Algunas   Algunos**   vestidos son azules.

4   **Nadie   Alguno**   tiene dinero.

SMART TIPS

- Use the word *igual* (equal, same) when comparing items with the same price.

  La camisa cuesta igual que los pantalones. (The shirt costs the same as the pants).

- *Alguno* and *ninguno* must agree with the noun in gender and number. Although they are frequently used as adjectives, they can also be used as nouns.

€100

€45

€20

€60

Activity A

As you've learned, reflexive verbs are used when applying action to oneself. Look at the sentences and rewrite them using the reflexive construction. Remember to include the reflexive pronoun with the verbs.

1 Yo pruebo la falda.

_____

2 Ellas visten en la mañana.

_____

3 Nosotros probamos los pantalones.

_____

4 Él viste con el mismo color.

_____

Challenge

Divertirse (to have fun) is an important irregular reflexive verb. Except for *nosotros/nosotras*, when conjugating, the e becomes *ie*. Try to complete the conjugation chart.

yo	me	
tú	te	diviertes
usted	se	
él/ella	se	
nosotros/ nosotras	nos	divertimos
ustedes	se	
ellos/ellas	se	

Activity B

Conjugate the verb *costar* (for help, refer to Lesson 6) and tell which items are more and less expensive. Write two sentences for each pair, one using *más que* and another with *menos que*.

Activity C

Based on the images, complete the crossword puzzle using the correct Spanish term. Remember to include the definite article for all nouns.

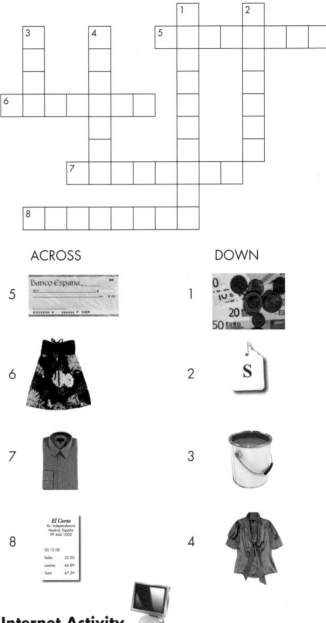

ACROSS

5

6

7

8

DOWN

1

2

3

4

Internet Activity

Go to **www.berlitzbooks.com/5minute** for a list of Spanish-language online shops to browse. Navigate each site and look at what is featured. Some sites may have different pages for *Mujeres* or *Hombres*. What is your favorite *camisa*? What is your favorite *chaqueta*? If you don't mind paying international shipping fees, go ahead and make a purchase!

Unit 8 Travel and Holidays

In this unit you will:
- ask for directions.
- talk about location.
- discuss an itinerary.
- use the irregular verbs *ir* (to go) and *conocer* (to know a person or place).

LESSON 1
¿Dónde está la estación?

Dialogue

A couple from Mexico is visiting Spain for the first time. They are looking for directions so they can get to the tourist office in *la Plaza Mayor*. Listen as Guillermo and Luz discuss where to go.

Luz Nosotros estamos aquí, en el Mercado de San Miguel. ¿Cómo llegamos a la oficina de turismo en la Plaza Mayor?

Guillermo Mira el mapa. La Plaza Mayor está en el centro de Madrid. Quiero tomar el autobús o el metro.

Luz No estamos lejos del centro. Vamos a caminar.

Guillermo El metro está cerca. Está delante de esa escuela.

Luz No, mejor vamos a caminar. Así, conocemos las calles y los edificios de Madrid. Quiero ver la biblioteca y las iglesias viejas.

Guillermo Está bien. ¡Vámonos!

SMART TIPS

- *¡Vámonos!* is a very common term in Spanish. It means "Let's go!"
- To encourage someone to do something use *Vamos*. For example: *vamos a pedir instrucciones* (let's ask for directions), *vamos a preguntar cómo llegar* (let's ask how to get there) or *vamos a conseguir una guía* (let's get a guide).

Activity A

Look at the clues. Try to guess the meaning of the following verbs. Write the English verb on the line.

llegar _____

tomar _____

caminar _____

Activity B

Answer the following questions in Spanish. If you don't know a word, try to figure out the meaning through the context of the dialogue, then look at the Words to Know page to check your vocabulary.

1 Where are Guillermo and Luz? _____

2 Where do they want to go? _____

3 How can they get there? _____

4 Why does Luz want to walk? _____

Core Words

Lugares (Places)

la biblioteca	library
la escuela	school
la estación de metro	subway station
la estación de tren	train station
la iglesia	church
la oficina de correos	post office
la parada de autobús	bus stop
el supermercado	supermarket

Ubicación (Location)

cerca de	near
a la derecha	to the right
atrás de	behind
delante de	in front of
lejos de	far
a la izquierda	to the left

Extra Words

la cuadra	block
la esquina	corner

Activity A

Label each building, station or stop with the correct Spanish word.

library

subway station

school

church

train station

bus stop

post office

supermarket

SMART TIPS

- When talking about the position of things, use the verb *estar*. For example: *La escuela está cerca de la biblioteca* (The school is near the library).

- To indicate that something is to the left or right of something else, use the preposition *a* after the verb *está*. *La biblioteca está a la izquierda de la escuela* (The library is to the left of the school).

Activity B

Circle the appropriate term to describe where each thing is located.

1   La estación de metro está _____ de la biblioteca.

    a a la izquierda   **b a la derecha**

2   La escuela está _____ la estación de tren.

    a lejos de   **b cerca de**

3   El supermercado está _____ la biblioteca.

    a lejos de   **b cerca de**

4   La parada de autobús está _____ la iglesia.

    a atrás de   **b delante de**

Smart Phrases

Core Phrases

Vamos a conseguir un mapa.	Let's get a map.
¿Dónde está _____?	Where is _____?
¿Cómo llego a _____?	How do I get to _____?
Para ir a _____, tome el autobús número _____.	To get to_____, take bus number _____.
Quiero tomar el tren/autobús/metro.	I want to take the train/bus/subway.
La estación de tren está cerca de la escuela.	The train station is near the school.

Extra Phrases

Disculpe.	Excuse me.
Muchas gracias.	Thanks a lot.
De nada.	You're welcome.

Activity A

Look at each picture. Write in Spanish that you want to use that mode of transportation. Then ask where you can find the station or the stop.

1 _____
_____

2 _____
_____

3 _____
_____

Activity B

What do you say if you want to…

1 …ask where the train station is?
_____
_____

2 …ask how to get to the subway station?
_____
_____

3 …tell someone the train station is near the school?
_____
_____

4 …say "let's get a map"?
_____
_____

Activity C

You are helping a tourist with directions. He needs to go to the plaza. To get there, he has to go to the bus stop and take bus number 9. Then, to go to the church, he has to take the train. Read his questions and tell him what to do.

1 ¿Cómo llego a la Plaza Mayor?
_____
_____
_____

2 ¿Cómo llego a la iglesia?
_____
_____
_____

Your Turn

You want to go to the bus station. Ask—out loud—where it is and how to get there. Don't forget to be polite!

LESSON 4

Smart Grammar

The verb *ir* (to go)

The verb *ir* is irregular. The chart shows its conjugation in the present tense.

yo	voy	I go
tú	vas	you go
usted	va	you go
él/ella	va	he/she goes
nosotros/nosotras	vamos	we go
ustedes	van	you go
ellos/ellas	van	they go

Examples

Voy a la escuela.   I go to school.
Vamos al supermercado.   We go to the supermarket.

Activity A

Fill in the blanks with the correct form of *ir*.

1   Ellos _____ a la biblioteca.

2   Ella _____ a la iglesia.

3   Nosotros _____ a la oficina de correos.

4   Tú _____ a la estación de tren.

Activity B

To ask a question with the verb *ir*, use *A dónde* and the appropriate form of *ir*. Write questions for the following answers. Example: *Pilar y Julieta van al supermercado. ¿A dónde van Pilar y Julieta?*

1   Luisa va al restaurante. _____

2   Darío va a Cancún. _____

3   El avión va a Quito. _____

4   Mis tíos van a Cartagena. _____
    _____

Activity B

Write sentences with the verb *ir* to tell where you think someone will go. Remember to use the contraction *al* when needed.

1 _____
   _____
   _____

2 _____
   _____
   _____

3 _____
   _____
   _____

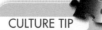

4 _____
   _____
   _____

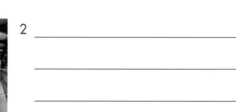

CULTURE TIP

If you are traveling from city to city in Spain, airfare can be expensive. A good alternative between big cities is the train system. It's reliable, fast and easy, and you may even make a friend along the way. The word for "ticket" in Spain is *billete*. *Billetes por favor* means "Tickets please." Other Spanish-speaking countries may use the word *boleto*.

Llegadas y salidas

Arrivals and Departures

Read the e-mail from Darío to Enrico with information about their trip to Cancun. Then answer the questions below.

Fecha:	Martes, 26 de agosto
De:	Darío
Para:	Enrico
Asunto:	Cancún

¡Hola Enrico!
¡Por fin vamos de vacaciones!
¡Vamos a Cancún!
¿Conoces Cancún? Yo no lo conozco.
Ya tengo los boletos de avión y la reservación del hotel. Mi maleta ya está lista.
Esta es la información: El vuelo es el número 12-35. Vamos desde Dallas hasta México. El avión sale de Dallas a las 11 de la mañana y llega a Cancún, México a las 6 de la tarde. Del aeropuerto de Cancún vamos en autobús hasta el hotel.
Nos vemos en el aeropuerto.
Hasta luego,
Darío

SMART TIPS

- The prepositions *de* and *desde* are both equivalent to the word "from" in English. They are interchangeable for the most part, however, *desde* is more often used with *hasta* in the context of moving from place to place. For example: *Voy desde el aeropuerto hasta la estación* or *Voy del* (*de + el*) *aeropuerto a la estación* (I go from the airport to the station).

- The preposition *a* means "to" in English. When the preposition is followed by the article *el*, combine them to form a contraction. *Llego al* (*a + el*) *hotel a las 3:00* (I arrive at the hotel at 3:00).

- You use *ya* to mean "already." *Ya tengo los boletos* (I already have the tickets).

Activity A

Circle the correct answer for each question.

1. Where are Darío and Enrico going?
   a Dallas   **b Cancun**

2. Do they have a hotel reservation?
   a no   **b yes**

3. What time does the plane leave Dallas?
   a 11 AM   **b 6 PM**

4. How are they getting to the hotel from the airport?
   a by bus   **b by car**

Activity B

Darío and Enrico's flight itinerary of *llegadas* and *salidas* has changed. Look at the new information and complete Darío's e-mail.

Mexico Airlines			MA639
Departs	**Time**	**Arrives**	**Time**
Dallas Fort Worth International Airport	10:00	Benito Juárez International Airport Mexico City	13:00
Benito Juárez International Airport Mexico City	16:00	Cancun International Airport	17:00

Fecha:	Miércoles, 27 de agosto
De:	Darío
Para:	Enrico
Asunto:	Cancún

Hola Enrico,
Tengo información nueva para el vuelo de mañana. El vuelo sale de Dallas a _____. Llegamos a la Ciudad de México a _____ y a Cancún a _____.

Words to Know

Core Words

el aeropuerto	airport
el avión	plane
el boleto	ticket
el equipaje	luggage
la maleta	suitcase
el pasaporte	passport
las vacaciones	vacation
el viaje	trip
el vuelo	flight

Extra Words

el hotel	hotel
la parada	stop/layover
la reservación	reservation

CULTURE TIP

While in Latin America you use the word *la visa* to refer to your visa, in Spain you use *el visado*.

SMART TIP

In Spanish, although the singular form *la vacación* exists, it's more common to use the plural form of the word: *Voy de vacaciones a España* (I'm going on vacation to Spain).

Activity A

Draw a line to match each picture with the correct Spanish word.

1

    a el pasaporte

2

    b el boleto

3

    c el avión

4

    d la maleta

5

    e el aeropuerto

Activity B

Pick the correct Spanish term from the choices below.

1 luggage
   a el equipaje   **b** el pasaporte   **c** la visa

2 flight
   a el vuelo   **b** la maleta   **c** el avión

3 trip
   a las vacaciones   **b** el viaje   **c** el boleto

4 vacation
   a el viaje   **b** las vacaciones   **c** el equipaje

Smart Phrases

C21, C22, C23
C24, C25, C26 Gates

Core Phrases

¿Cuándo sale el próximo vuelo a Cancún?	When is the next flight to Cancun?
¿De qué puerta sale?	Which is the departing gate?
¿A qué sala llega?	Which is the arriving gate?
El vuelo sale a la/las ____.	The flight leaves at ____.
El avión llega a la/las ____.	The plane arrives at ____.
¿Cuánto cuesta el vuelo?	How much does the flight cost?
El vuelo cuesta 500 dólares de ida y vuelta.	The flight costs $500 round-trip.

Extra Phrases

¡Por fin!	At last!
Nos vemos en _____.	I'll see you at _____.

Activity A

What do you say if you want to…

1   …tell your friend that your flight leaves at 12:30?

_____

2   …ask which is the departing gate?

_____

3   …ask which is the arriving gate?

_____

Activity B

Armando is looking for the next available flight to Cancun. He goes up to a ticket agent and asks him a few questions. Circle the best responses to Armando's questions.

1   ¿Cuándo sale el próximo vuelo a Cancún?

   a El vuelo sale a las ocho.

   b El avión llega a las dos.

2   ¿Cuánto cuesta el vuelo?

   a El avión llega a las dos.

   b El vuelo cuesta 500 dólares de ida y vuelta.

3   Quiero ese vuelo. ¿De qué puerta sale?

   a La puerta A5.

   b El vuelo sale a las ocho.

Activity C

Look at the chart and answer the questions below.

SALIDAS		
Hora	Destino	Vuelo
16:15	Quito	EZY5258
16:35	Cartagena	EZY5259
17:00	Madrid	MZY448058
17:00	Veracruz	VZX7250
17:20	Puebla	VZX7251
17:25	Lima	LNN4432

1   ¿A qué hora sale el próximo vuelo a Puebla?

_____

2   ¿Qué vuelos salen a las 5:00 de la tarde?

_____

Your Turn

You work for Iberia Airlines and you have to announce the next flight to Madrid: Flight 1699, departs at 10:23 AM, arrives at 1:30 PM. Use your new phrases and vocabulary to give information about the flight.

CULTURE TIP

Ida y vuelta means "round-trip" or "return." *Ida* means one-way. In Mexico, you say *sencillo* (one way) and *redondo* (round-trip).

SMART PRONUNCIATION

To say 500 in Spanish, you say *quinientos*. Note that *q* in Spanish sounds like the *k* in "kick": kee•<u>neeyehn</u>•tohs.

Smart Grammar

The verb *conocer* (to know)

The verb *conocer* is irregular. The chart shows its conjugations in the present tense.

yo	conozco	I know
tú	conoces	you know
usted	conoce	you know
él/ella	conoce	he/she knows
nosotros/nosotras	conocemos	we know
ustedes	conocen	you know
ellos/ellas	conocen	they know

Examples

Conozco a Tatiana. — I know Tatiana.
Ellos conocen Barcelona. — They know Barcelona.
No conozco Veracruz. — I don't know Veracruz.

SMART TIP

While the Spanish verb *conocer* literally translates as "to know," it usually means "to be familiar with," and it should be applied to people and places, not to facts, skills or ideas. The verb meaning "to know" for facts and ideas is *saber*. *Saber* is irregular only in the *yo* form.

For example:
Yo sé hablar español.
(I know how to speak Spanish.)
Nosotros sabemos nadar.
(We know how to swim.)

Activity A

Conjugate the verb *conocer* for each sentence.

1 ¿ _____ New York?
   tú
2 No _____ España.
   yo
3 _____ a la madre de Pedro.
   nosotros
4 ¿ _____ a María?
   ustedes

Direct Object Pronouns

me	me
te	you
lo	him/it (m)
la	her/it (f)
nos	us
los	you (pl.)/them (m)
las	you (pl.)/them (f)

Examples

Luis me conoce. — Luis knows me.
Yo los tengo. — I have them.
Te conozco. — I know you.

Activity B

Change the sentences so they use direct object pronouns.

1 Yo bebo el vino. _____
2 Ella estudia inglés. _____
3 Tú conoces las casas. _____
4 Ellos llevan los boletos. _____

Your Turn

Do you know them? Look at each picture and write a sentence using *conocer* to indicate if you know or don't know each person, place or animal. Remember to use direct object pronouns.

1   ¿Los conoce?

2

_____   _____

3

4

_____   _____

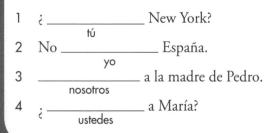

Activity A

Read Paco's postcard from his trip to Ecuador. He didn't conjugate the verbs *ir* and *conocer* correctly. Cross out the mistakes and rewrite the verbs using the correct form.

Querida Clara,

Mi madre y yo estamos en Ecuador. Nosotros vas a Quito mañana. ¿Tú conocen Quito? Yo lo conoces bien. Después va a Venezuela. ¿Conocen Venezuela?

Un abrazo,

Paco

Activity B

Fill in the blanks to complete Toni's plan for her trip to Madrid.

Mi viaje a Madrid

_____ a Madrid, España. _____
   I go   My flight leaves at
las ocho de la mañana. Llego _____
                              at the airport
a las seis. ¡Es muy temprano! Tengo mi _____,
                                        ticket
_____ y _____. Llego a Madrid a las diez
 luggage   passport
de la mañana y busco _____ para ir al hotel.
                     a train station
El hotel está _____ Centro de Arte Reina Sofía.
              near the
Yo lo conozco. También está _____.
                            behind a church
Mañana, _____ para ir al Palacio
        I want to take the subway
Real. Necesito un billete de metro. Ah, ya lo tengo.

Activity C

Augusto and Gabriela are visiting Chile. They are looking for the post office. Write the correct Spanish word or phrase to complete their dialogue.

Augusto ¿_____ la oficina de correos?
             Where is

Gabriela _____ un mapa.
             Let's get

Augusto Mira el mapa. La oficina de correos está _____.
            to the right of the library

Gabriela Sí, y también está _____.
                               behind the supermarket

Augusto Esta es _____.
                    the bus stop

Gabriela Sí. Ahí _____ tomamos.
                     it

Challenge

As you know, *saber* also means "to know," but it's used with facts, ideas and knowing how to do things. *Saber* is irregular, but all the conjugations except for *yo* follow the regular –er verb rules. Can you complete the chart?

yo	_____
tú	_____
usted	_____
él/ella	_____
nosotros/nosotras	_____
ustedes	_____
ellos/ellas	_____

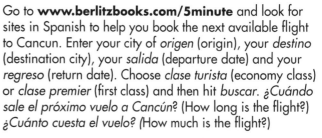

Internet Activity

Go to **www.berlitzbooks.com/5minute** and look for sites in Spanish to help you book the next available flight to Cancun. Enter your city of *origen* (origin), your *destino* (destination city), your *salida* (departure date) and your *regreso* (return date). Choose *clase turista* (economy class) or *clase premier* (first class) and then hit *buscar*. ¿Cuándo sale el próximo vuelo a Cancún? (How long is the flight?) ¿Cuánto cuesta el vuelo? (How much is the flight?)

Unit 9　Professions

In this unit you will:
- **describe different professions.**
- **compare different jobs.**
- **read a job application in Spanish.**
- **conjugate regular verbs in the past and future tenses.**

LESSON 1

Entrevista de trabajo

> **SMART TIP**
>
> *Sobre* (about) can be used with the verb *ser* to talk about the topic or theme of a book, movie or article. Example: *El artículo es sobre economía* (The article is about economy).
>
> The verb *tratar* (literally, to treat) with the preposition *de* can also be used. Example: *El libro trata de la vida de Gabriel García Márquez* (The book is about Gabriel García Márquez's life).

Dialogue

Rosalina is on a job interview for *El Diario de Latinoamérica*, a famous newspaper. Listen as her potential employer asks about her previous job and responsibilities.

Empleador ¿Dónde trabajó antes?

Rosalina Trabajé en un periódico, *El Vocero*.

Empleador ¿Escribió artículos para ese periódico?

Rosalina Sí. Escribí varios artículos.

Empleador ¿Sobre qué son los artículos?

Rosalina Son sobre la cultura en Latinoamérica. Aquí están los artículos.

Empleador ¡Estos artículos son muy buenos! Estás contratada.

Rosalina ¡Muchas gracias! ¿Cuándo empiezo?

Empleador El próximo lunes. Te veo el lunes a las ocho.

> **SMART PRONUNCIATION**
>
> In Spanish, the *j* is pronounced like the *h* in the word "hot." The *h* sound is a bit stronger in Spanish, in the back of the throat, so *trabajar* is pronounced trah•bah•<u>khar</u>.

Activity A

Circle the correct answer for each question.

1　Where did Rosalina work before?

　　a revista　　**b periódico**

2　What did Rosalina do at her previous job?

　　a enseñó　　**b escribió**

3　What does Rosalina show the employer?

　　a fotos　　**b artículos**

4　Does Rosalina get the job?

　　a sí　　**b no**

Activity B

Choose a word from the box to complete each sentence.

> escribió　　cultura　　empieza　　trabajó

1　Rosalina _____ en un periódico.

2　Rosalina _____ artículos para un periódico.

3　Escribió artículos sobre _____.

4　Rosalina _____ el lunes a las ocho.

Words to Know

Core Words

el estudiante/la estudiante	student (m/f)
la oficina	office
el periódico	newspaper
el periodista/la periodista	journalist (m/f)
la profesión	profession
el profesor/la profesora	teacher or professor (m/f)
la revista	magazine
el salón	classroom

Extra Words

el artículo	article
el empleador	employer

SMART TIP

Unlike most Spanish nouns, you cannot tell the gender of the word *estudiante* by its ending. Instead, you should look at its article or the context. This is also true for the words *periodista* (journalist), *recepcionista* (receptionist) and *artista* (artist).

CULTURE TIP

You can identify daily newspapers in Latin America and Spain by the word *Diario* in the name. There's *El Diario Colatino* from El Salvador, *El Diario de México* from Mexico, *El Diario del Cusco* from Peru and *El Diario de Mallorca* from Spain, among many others.

Activity A

Fill in the blanks with the correct Spanish word to complete the diary entry.

Querido diario,

Estoy en un _____.

classroom

_____ está hablando de un artículo

The teacher

en el periódico. Hay muchos _____

students

en mi clase. No quiero estar aquí. Quiero ser una

_____ para una _____.

journalist　　　　　　　　magazine

No quiero ser una _____.

student

Activity B

Label each picture with the appropriate Spanish words and articles.

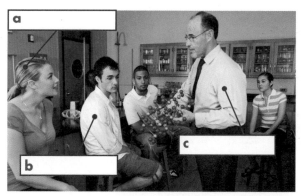

Smart Phrases

Core Phrases

¿Cuál es su profesión? — What's your profession?
Soy un periodista/una periodista. — I'm a journalist. (m/f)
Soy un profesor/una profesora. — I'm a teacher. (m/f)
¿Qué quiere ser? — What do you want to be?
Quiero ser un profesor/una profesora. — I want to be a professor. (m/f)

Extra Phrases

Te veo el lunes. — I'll see you on Monday.
Nos vemos el lunes. — We'll see each other on Monday.

Estás contratado/contratada. — You're hired. (m/f)

Activity A

¿Cuál es su profesión? Look at the pictures and complete the sentences to tell the person's profession.

El Diario

1 Soy _____   2 Soy _____

¿Qué quiere ser? Now look at the pictures and decide what each person wants to be. Write the answer on the blanks below.

3 _____   4 _____

Activity B

What do you say if you want to…

1 …ask someone what he or she wants to be?

_____

2 …say you want to be a professor?

_____

3 …ask someone about his or her profession?

_____

4 …say you're a journalist?

_____

Your Turn

Imagine you are a journalist. You're meeting a professor for the first time. Tell her your current profession and ask about hers. Then use the words *diseñador/diseñadora de moda* (fashion designer), *escritor/escritora* (writer) or *reportero/reportera* (reporter) to tell her what you want to be.

Write your sentences for more practice.

_____
_____
_____
_____
_____
_____
_____
_____
_____
_____

Smart Grammar

SMART TIP

Another way to form the past tense in Spanish is to use the verb *haber* before a verb with a new ending (*-ado* for *-ar* verbs and *-ido* for *-er* and *-ir* verbs). This is more common in Spain than in Latin America. For example, *Me he divertido* (I've had fun) is often used in Spain while *Me divertí* is more common in Latin America.

Regular Verbs in the Past Tense

Verbs with *-ar*

Drop the *-ar* and add the appropriate ending for each pronoun, such as with *trabajar* (to work).

yo	trabaj**é**	I worked
tú	trabaj**aste**	you worked
usted	trabaj**ó**	you worked
él/ella	trabaj**ó**	he/she worked
nosotros/nosotras	trabaj**amos**	we worked
ustedes	trabaj**aron**	you worked
ellos/ellas	trabaj**aron**	they worked

Verbs with *-er* and *-ir*

Drop the *-er* or *-ir* and add the appropriate ending for each pronoun, such as with *aprender* (to learn) and *escribir* (to write).

yo	aprend**í**	I learned
tú	aprend**iste**	you learned
usted	aprend**ió**	you learned
él/ella	aprend**ió**	he/she learned
nosotros/nosotras	aprend**imos**	we learned
ustedes	aprend**ieron**	you learned
ellos/ellas	aprend**ieron**	they learned

yo	escrib**í**	I wrote
tú	escrib**iste**	you wrote
usted	escrib**ió**	you wrote
él/ella	escrib**ió**	he/she wrote
nosotros/nosotras	escrib**imos**	we wrote
ustedes	escrib**ieron**	you wrote
ellos/ellas	escrib**ieron**	they wrote

Activity A

Complete the sentences with the past tense of the verb in parentheses.

1 Tú _____ ocho horas ayer (yesterday).
    trabajar

2 Ella _____ mucho el mes pasado (last month).
    aprender

3 El año pasado (last year), nosotros _____ un artículo de periódico.
    escribir

4 Ellos _____ la semana pasada (last week).
    trabajar

Activity B

Rewrite the following sentences in the past tense.

1 Yo trabajo en la oficina.

   _____

2 Ustedes aprenden inglés.

   _____

3 Él vive en Panamá.

   _____

4 Tú comes pollo.

   _____

5 Ella escribe un artículo.

   _____

6 Mariana y yo escribimos una tarjeta postal.

   _____

LESSON 5

Solicitud de trabajo

SMART TIPS

To help you understand a text or a conversation:

- Remember to look for cognates—Spanish words that are similar or the same in English. For example: *editorial, secretario, educación, banco, asistente* and *especialización*.
- Look for roots of words you know. For example: You know that the words *periodista* and *periódico* mean "journalist" and "newspaper." *Periodismo*, used in the application, has the same root and means "journalism." *Trabajo* has the same root as the verb *trabajar* and it means "job" or "work."

A Job Application

Raúl is applying for *un puesto de corrector* (proofreader position) at *El Diario de la Costa del Sol. Algún día* (some day) he wants to be a journalist. Look at his *solicitud* (application form).

Solicitud de trabajo para
El Diario de la Costa del Sol

Raúl Ortiz	826.902.2703
Nombre	Número de teléfono
Ave. Andalucía 25, Málaga 29006, España	
Dirección	

EDUCACIÓN

Escuela	Especialización	Desde – Hasta
Universidad de Madrid	Periodismo	2002 – 2004

HISTORIAL DE TRABAJO

Banco Popular	secretario
Empleador/Empleadora	Puesto
junio 2004 – septiembre 2005	Luis Ramírez
Desde – Hasta	Jefe/Jefa

Periódico Metro Málaga	asistente editorial
Empleador/Empleadora	Puesto
noviembre 2008 – presente	José Velasquez
Desde – Hasta	Jefe/Jefa

Sueldo en el último trabajo: €22,000

Sueldo deseado: €27,000

Puesto deseado: corrector

¿Por qué desea este puesto?

Porque algún día quiero ser periodista. En el periódico Metro Málaga aprendí mucho. Como corrector aprenderé más.

Activity A

Complete the sentences with information from the application.

1 Raul Ortiz is applying for a position as _____ _____.

2 He studied journalism at the University of Madrid for _____ years.

3 His first job was at _____.

4 From November 2008 to the present he has worked for _____.

5 He thinks he will learn more if he works for _____.

Activity B

The verb *desear* means the same as *querer* (to want). Can you guess the meaning of these words?

1 puesto deseado _____

2 sueldo deseado _____

SMART TIP

Por qué as two words with an accent on the e means "why." *Porque* as one word with no accent means "because." Examples: *¿Por qué quieres trabajar aquí?* (Why do you want to work here?) *Quiero trabajar aquí porque me interesa la historia* (I want to work here because I'm interested in history).

Core Words

el asistente/la asistente	assistant (m/f)
el empleado/la empleada	employee (m/f)
el jefe/la jefa	boss (m/f)
el secretario/la secretaria	secretary (m/f)
el sueldo	salary
el trabajo	job

Extra Words

la compañía	company
el negocio	business
fácil	easy
difícil	difficult
mucho	a lot

Activity A

Circle the word that best answers each question.

1   Which word is not a type of job?

   a asistente   **b secretario**   **c sueldo**

2   Which word doesn't change its ending in the feminine form?

   a asistente   **b jefe**   **c secretario**

3   Which person pays your salary?

   a corrector   **b jefe**   **c asistente**

4   What do you call the amount of money you get paid for your work?

   a empleado   **b sueldo**   **c trabajo**

Activity B

Read the clues and complete the crossword with vocabulary from the Core Words.

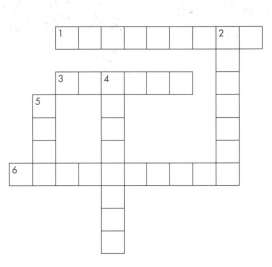

Across

1   Una persona que asiste (assists).

3   Pago por mi trabajo.

6   Esta persona organiza (organizes) las cosas en la oficina. (m)

Down

2   Soy periodista. Es mi _____.

4   Él trabaja para mí. Es mi _____.

5   Esta persona me paga el sueldo. (m)

Your Turn

Imagine you have your own *compañía*. Create a list of the people you need to hire. How many *empleados*? How many of those will be *asistentes* and *secretarios*? What is the *sueldo* for each *empleado*?

Smart Phrases

Core Phrases

¿Por qué desea este puesto?	Why do you want this position?
Porque quiero ser periodista.	Because I want to be a journalist.
Me gusta ayudar.	I like to help.
Me gusta escribir.	I like to write.
¿Cuánto tiempo ha trabajado allí?	How long have you worked there?
Trabajo allí hace tres meses.	I have worked there for three months.
es más fácil que	it's easier than
es más difícil que	it's harder than

Extra Phrases

paga más	it pays more
paga menos	it pays less

SMART TIP

To say what activities you like, use *me gusta* and add a verb in the infinitive form. For example: *Me gusta jugar* (I like to play), *Me gusta cantar* (I like to sing), *Me gusta leer* (I like to read).

Activity A

ingeniero	engineer
abogado	lawyer
constructor	builder

What do you think? Write *más fácil* or *más difícil* to compare each pair of jobs.

1 El trabajo de doctor es _____ que el trabajo de dentista.

2 El trabajo de profesor es _____ que el trabajo de ingeniero.

3 El trabajo de periodista es _____ que el trabajo de abogado.

4 El trabajo de constructor es _____ que el trabajo de diseñador de moda.

Activity B

What do you say if you want to...

1 ...ask someone why he or she wants to be a journalist?

_____

_____

2 ...tell someone you like to help?

_____

_____

3 ...ask someone how long he or she has worked somewhere?

_____

_____

4 ...tell someone that you have worked somewhere for two years?

_____

_____

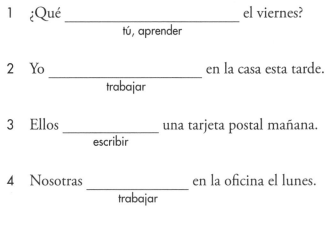

Regular Verbs in the Future Tense

All regular verbs use the same endings in the future form. Add the ending to *–ar, –er* and *–ir* verbs to form the future.

yo	trabajar**é**	I will work
tú	trabajar**ás**	you will work
usted	trabajar**á**	you will work
él/ella	trabajar**á**	he/she will work
nosotros/nosotras	trabajar**emos**	we will work
ustedes	trabajar**án**	you will work
ellos/ellas	trabajar**án**	they will work

Examples:

No trabajaremos la próxima semana.

We will not work next week.

Aprenderé más mañana.

I will learn more tomorrow.

¿Cuándo escribirás el libro?

When will you write the book?

SMART TIP

All the verbs in the future tense except those conjugated with *nosotros/nosotras* have accents on the last syllable.

Activity A

Complete the sentences by writing the future tense of the verb. Be sure to read the entire sentence for its context.

1 ¿Qué _____ el viernes?
tú, aprender

2 Yo _____ en la casa esta tarde.
trabajar

3 Ellos _____ una tarjeta postal mañana.
escribir

4 Nosotras _____ en la oficina el lunes.
trabajar

Activity B

This is Elena's wish list for next year. Use the future tense to tell what she will do.

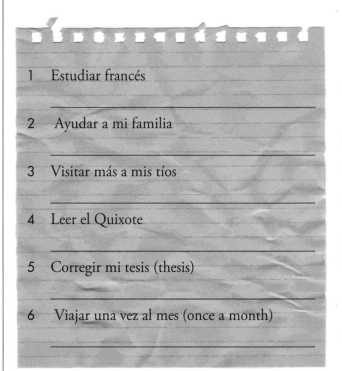

1 Estudiar francés

_____

2 Ayudar a mi familia

_____

3 Visitar más a mis tíos

_____

4 Leer el Quixote

_____

5 Corregir mi tesis (thesis)

_____

6 Viajar una vez al mes (once a month)

_____

Activity A

Use the clues to complete the crossword puzzle. If the answer is a noun, be sure to include the correct definite article.

ACROSS	DOWN
3 teacher (f)	1 secretary (m)
4 student (m)	2 boss (f)
6 magazine	5 salary

Activity B

Complete the questions using the correct past or future conjugation for each verb.

1 ¿Cuándo _____?

Ellos trabajarán el sábado.

2 ¿Cuándo _____?

Aprendí la canción ayer.

3 ¿Qué _____?

Ella escribió un artículo para la revista *Semana*.

Activity C

Now write the missing question or answer in each exchange.

1 ¿Cuándo viajará Ernesto a San Cristóbal?

_____

2 ¿Dónde veremos a Luis?

_____

3 _____

El estudiante escribirá su artículo mañana.

4 _____

Ellos cocinarán una pizza para la cena.

Activity D

The following sentences contain a mistake. Rewrite the sentences to correct the mistakes.

1 ¿Dónde trabajaste mañana?

_____

2 Por que quiero ayudar a la gente.

_____

3 Deseo este trabajo por qué es más fácil.

_____

4 Laura y Lola escriben en el artículo ayer.

_____

> ## Challenge
>
> What's another Spanish word for *sueldo*? _____
>
> What's another Spanish word for *puesto*? _____

Internet Activity

Go to **www.berlitzbooks.com/5minute** for a list of Spanish-language job search engines to browse. How many *asistente* positions can you find? What about *secretarios* and *abogados*? What are the *sueldos* like for each position?

Unit 10 At Home/Going Out

In this unit you will:

- talk about things to do around a house or an apartment.
- use the imperative form to give orders and instructions.
- use expressions for going out at night.
- use vocabulary about places to go.
- learn the past tense of the verbs *ir* and *ser.*

LESSON 1

¡Ayúdame!

Elisa's E-mail

Elisa writes an e-mail to her brother Domingo. She asks him to help her clean her apartment. (Notice how they are using the informal because they are related.)

```
⊝ ⊝ ⊝
Fecha:    Martes, 26 de agosto
De:       Elisa
Para:     Domingo
Asunto:   ¡Ayúdame!
```
```
Hola Domingo,
¿Puedes ayudarme con mi apartamento?
Papá y mamá llegarán mañana y el
apartamento está un poco desordenado.
Quiero recoger la ropa y organizar el
armario del baño. Después, quiero
limpiar los cuartos y pintar mi
dormitorio.
¿Cómo me puedes ayudar? Tú recoges la
ropa y yo organizo el armario. Después,
limpiamos y pintamos juntos.
¿Te parece mi plan?
¡Ayúdame por favor!
Un abrazo,
Elisa
```

desordenado	messy	recoger	to pick up
limpiar	to clean	pintar	to paint
No te preocupes.	Don't worry.	juntos	together

Activity A

Circle the correct answer for each question.

1. What does Elisa need help with?
   a her house **b her apartment**

2. Who will visit Elisa tomorrow?
   a her parents **b her aunt and uncle**

3. What does Elisa ask Domingo to do?
   a organize her closet **b pick up her clothes**

4. What does Elisa suggest they do together?
   a organize her closet **b paint**

Activity B

```
⊝ ⊝ ⊝
Fecha:    Martes, 26 de agosto
De:       Domingo
Para:     Elisa
Asunto:   ¡Ayúdame!
```
```
Hola Elisa,
Sí, puedo ayudarte. Pero, no quiero
recoger tu ropa. Tú recoge la ropa y yo
organizo el armario. Después, limpiamos
y pintamos juntos.
No te preocupes. Yo te ayudo.
Nos vemos pronto,
Domingo
```

Read Domingo's response. Then answer the questions in Spanish.

1. Is Domingo going to help Elisa?
   _____

2. What doesn't Domingo want to do?
   _____

3. What does Domingo want to do?
   _____

4. What does Domingo say that he and Elisa can do together?
   _____

Words to Know

Core Words

el apartamento	apartment
el armario	closet
el baño	bathroom
la cocina	kitchen
el comedor	dining room
el cuarto	room
el dormitorio	bedroom
la sala	living room

Extra Words

las escaleras	stairs
el jardín	garden
el suelo	floor
la ventana	window

Activity A

Fill in the blanks with the correct Spanish words to complete the dialogue. For the *yo* part of the dialogue, answer the questions based on your own home.

Amigo ¿Vives en una casa o en _____?

Yo Vivo en _____.

Amigo ¿Cuántos _____ hay?
rooms

Yo Hay _____.

Amigo ¿Cuáles son _____ más grandes?
the rooms

Yo Los cuartos mas grandes son _____

_____ .

Activity B

Look at each picture. Then choose the correct word from the box to name each picture.

el baño	el dormitorio	la sala
la cocina	el comedor	el armario

1 _____   2 _____

3 _____   4 _____

5 _____   6 _____

CULTURE TIP

The words *dormitorio* and *cuarto* can be used interchangeably to mean "bedroom." In Mexico, however, people also use the word *recámara*. Other words for "bedroom" in Latin America include *alcoba, aposento, pieza, habitación, habitación de dormir* and *cuarto de dormir*.

LESSON 3

Smart Phrases

Core Phrases

¿Puedes ayudarme?	Can you help me?
Sí, puedo ayudarte.	Yes, I can help you.
No, no puedo ayudarte.	No, I can't help you.
¿Qué quieres que haga?	What do you want me to do?
Ahora mismo.	Right away.

Extra Phrases

¡Ayúdame por favor!	Help me please!
¿Te parece mi plan?	Do you like my plan?
Nos vemos pronto.	See you soon.
un abrazo	hugs

SMART TIP

Did you notice the informal "you" was used in the phrases above? That's because the correspondence in Lesson 1 was between siblings. Remember to use the formal when speaking to all but family, friends and children.

Activity A

What do you say if you want to…

1   …ask someone to help you?

   _____

2   …say that you can't help someone?

   _____

3   …ask what someone wants you to do?

   _____

4   …say "right away"?

   _____

Activity B

Put the dialogue in order. Number the phrases 1–4.

Sí, puedo ayudarte.
¿Qué quieres que haga?

#

Recoge la ropa.

#

Ahora mismo.

#

¿Puedes ayudarme?

#

Smart Grammar

The verb *poder* (can, to be able)

The verb *poder* is irregular. The chart shows its conjugation in the present tense.

yo	puedo	I can
tú	puedes	you can
usted	puede	you can
él/ella	puede	he/she can
nosotros/nosotras	podemos	we can
ustedes	pueden	you can
ellos/ellas	pueden	they can

Activity A

What can each of these people do? Write the correct form of the verb *poder* in the blanks.

1 Tú _____ escribir.

2 Él _____ cantar.

3 Ellos _____ limpiar.

4 Ella _____ pintar.

Commands

Spanish commands are verb forms used to give an order. These are the most common command forms for –*ar* and –*er* verbs. Remember to drop the pronoun since the verb form indicates the person spoken to.

ayudar	to help
¡Tú ayuda!	Help! (sing.,inf.)
¡Usted ayude!	Help! (sing., form.)
¡Ustedes ayuden!	Help! (pl.)
recoger	to pick up
¡Tú recoge!	Pick up! (sing., inf.)
¡Usted recoja!	Pick up! (sing., form.)
¡Ustedes recojan!	Pick up! (pl.)

Activity B

Roxana needs to get things done around the house. She asks her family to help out. Use the given verbs and nouns to write each command.

recoger/tu ropa

pintar/el cuarto

organizar/el armario

limpiar/el suelo

¿A dónde fuiste?

SMART TIP

Fuiste, fue, fuimos and *fui* are the past tense forms of the verbs *ir* and *ser* for *tú, él/ella, nosotros* and *yo*, respectively. You will learn more about these conjugations in Lesson 8.

Diary Entry

Read Catalina's diary entry about where she went this week.

> Querido diario,
>
> Ésta fue una buena semana. Anteayer mis amigos y yo fuimos a un concierto de rock. Nos divertimos mucho. Ayer mi madre y yo fuimos a la tienda a comprar ropa. Después fui al club con mi novio y bailamos toda la noche. ¡Quiero bailar otra vez muy pronto!

nos divertimos	we had fun
toda la noche	all night
otra vez	again
muy pronto	very soon

Activity A

Circle the correct answer for each question.

1   What did Catalina do the day before yesterday?

  a went to the concert   **b went to the club**

2   What did Catalina do yesterday?

  a went to the concert   **b went to the store**

3   What did Catalina do last night?

  a went to the club   **b went to the concert**

4   What does Catalina want to do again?

  a buy clothes   **b dance**

Activity B

Answer the following questions in Spanish.

1   How has Catalina's week been?

  _____

2   How was the concert the other day?

  _____

3   What did Catalina do after shopping?

  _____

4   Who did she go with?

  _____

Activity C

Write in Spanish what Catalina did each day.

1   anteayer

  _____

2   ayer

  _____

3   ayer en la noche

  _____

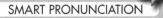

SMART PRONUNCIATION

Although *club* looks the same in Spanish as in English, it's pronounced differently. In Spanish, the *u* sounds like the *oo* in "food," so *club* is pronounced kloob.

LESSON 6
Words to Know

Core Words

anoche	last night
anteayer	day before yesterday
ayer	yesterday
la semana pasada	last week
bailar	to dance
el bar	bar
el cine	movie theater
el concierto	concert
la película	movie
el teatro	theater

Activity A
Where did the following people go last night? Look at the pictures and write the Spanish word for the place where each person went.

1 _____

2 _____

3 _____

4 _____

Activity B
Hoy es miércoles. Write *anoche, ayer, anteayer* or *la semana pasada* to tell when you did each activity.

1   Yo bailé el martes. _____

2   Fui al cine el lunes. _____

3   Fui al concierto el miércoles pasado. _____

4   Fui al bar el martes en la noche. _____

Activity C
Complete the crossword puzzle in Spanish using the English clue words.

ACROSS	DOWN
1 last night	1 day before yesterday
2 movie	3 movie theater
5 to dance	4 bar

> **SMART TIP**
>
> When referring to a particular movie, use *la película*. Say *Quiero ver la película* (I want to see the movie). However, if you want to go to the movies, use *el cine* and say *Quiero ir al cine.*

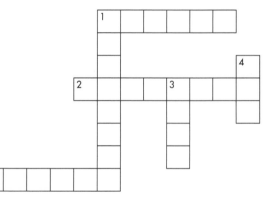

LESSON 7

Smart Phrases

Core Phrases

¿Qué hizo anoche/ ayer/anteayer/ la semana pasada?

What did you do last night/ yesterday/the day before yesterday/last week?

¿Qué quiere hacer? — What do you want to do?

Quiero quedarme en casa. — I want to stay in.

Quiero salir. — I want to go out.

Extra Phrases

Vamos a salir. — Let's go out.

Vamos a tomar un trago. — Let's have a drink.

Activity A

What do you say if you want to…

1   …ask what someone did last week?

   _____

2   …ask what someone wants to do?

   _____

3   …say you want to go out?

   _____

4   …say you want to stay in?

   _____

CULTURE TIP

Spain is known for its nightlife. People go out to dinner as late as 10 PM and stay out all night long. Often, clubs (also known as *discotecas*) and bars don't open until midnight and stay open until dawn. If in Spain, make use of the afternoon *siesta* (nap) to be ready for the night ahead.

Activity B

Eduardo wants to take Estrella out tonight. Estrella doesn't want to go out. Eduardo suggests activities, but to no avail. Put their dialogue in order to figure out what Eduardo decides to do. (Notice Eduardo uses the informal because Estrella is his friend.)

___ **Eduardo**   Pero, quiero salir de la casa. ¿Quieres bailar?

___ **Estrella**   Fui al cine anoche.

___ **Eduardo**   ¿Vamos al cine?

___ **Estrella**   Quiero quedarme en casa esta noche.

___ **Eduardo**   Nos quedamos en casa esta noche.

___ **Estrella**   Fui a bailar con mis amigos ayer.

_1_ **Eduardo**   ¿Qué quieres hacer esta noche?

Write in Spanish what Eduardo ultimately decides to do about the evening.

_____

_____

_____

_____

_____

_____

Your Turn

¿Qué quiere hacer esta noche?

_____

_____

_____

_____

_____

Past tense of verbs *ir* and *ser*

The verbs *ir* and *ser* are irregular. These two verbs are conjugated the same way in the past tense. Look for context clues to determine which verb is being used.

yo	fui	I went *or* was
tú	fuiste	you went *or* were
usted	fue	you went *or* were
él/ella	fue	he/she went *or* was
nosotros/nosotras	fuimos	we went *or* were
ustedes	fueron	you went *or* were
ellos/ellas	fueron	they went *or* were

Examples:

Ella fue a la tienda ayer.   She went to the store yesterday.

Él fue un estudiante durante el invierno.   He was a student during the winter.

Activity A

Determine whether the sentences use *ir* or *ser*. Write *ir* or *ser* on the line provided.

1   Fue al supermercado ayer. _____

2   La película no fue buena. _____

3   ¿A dónde fuiste anoche?   _____

4   Fueron buenos amigos.   _____

> **SMART TIP**
>
> If you see the prepositions *a* or *al* after the verb, you will know that the verb means "went" instead of "was."

Activity B

Write the correct form of *ir* or *ser* in the blanks.

1   Yo _____ a la casa de mi madre anoche.

2   Tú _____ al trabajo ayer.

3   Él _____ mi jefe por dos años.

4   Nosotras _____ al juego anteayer.

5   Ellos _____ novios durante el verano.

6   Mis abuelos _____ a Quito.

Activity C

Now see if you can translate the sentences in Activity B. Write the English version of the sentences on the lines provided.

1   _____

2   _____

3   _____

4   _____

5   _____

6   _____

Your Turn

¿A dónde fuiste anoche?

_____

¿A dónde fuiste anteayer?

_____

Activity A

Solve the following anagrams. Use the pictures as clues.

1 a ñ o b   _ _ _ _

2 u í l a l p e c   _ _ _ _ _ _ _ _

3 r i l b a a   _ _ _ _ _ _

4 t r a n i p   _ _ _ _ _ _

5 a c i n c o   _ _ _ _ _ _

Activity B

Circle the sentence that best completes Tina's answers.

1 **Jorge** ¿Qué quieres hacer esta noche?

   Tina Estoy cansada.
   a Escuché música anteayer.   **b Quiero quedarme en casa esta noche.**

2 **Jorge** ¡Quiero salir! Vamos a bailar.

   Tina No Jorge.
   a Bailé con Luis ayer.   **b Fui al cine anoche.**

3 **Jorge** ¿Quieres tomar una cerveza en el bar?

   Tina No.
   a Quiero salir de la casa.   **b Tomé cerveza esta tarde.**

4 **Jorge** ¿Y el cine? Podemos ver una película.

   Tina No.
   a No quiero salir de la casa.   **b ¿Qué hiciste anoche?**

Activity C

Answer the following questions in Spanish.

1 ¿A dónde fuiste con mi carro anoche?

   _____

2 ¿Cuál fue la película?

   _____

3 ¿Cuáles fueron los postres en el restaurante?

   _____

4 ¿Fueron ustedes al concierto?

   _____

Activity D

Use the imperative forms of the verb to write the following commands.

1 help me clean (tú): _____

2 help me paint (usted): _____

3 pick up your clothes (ustedes):
   _____

4 pick up that book (tú):
   _____

> **Challenge**
>
> Change the commands in Activity D into questions using the verb *poder*. For example, for number 1 you would ask: *¿Puedes ayudarme a limpiar?*

Internet Activity

Go to **www.berlitzbooks.com/5minute** for a list of forums where Spanish learners can chat with native Spanish speakers. Ask different people in the forum what they did *ayer, anoche, anteayer* and *la semana pasada.*

Unit 11 Body and Health

In this unit you will:
- learn vocabulary for body and health.
- use adverbs of time.
- describe common symptoms and ailments.
- use the future tense with *ir* + *a* + infinitive verb.

LESSON 1

Estoy enfermo

Dialogue

Melisa asks her friend Roberto to play tennis, but he's sick. They make an appointment for a different day. Listen to their conversation.

Roberto Hola, Melisa. ¿Qué vas a hacer hoy?

Melisa Voy a jugar tenis. ¿Quieres jugar?

Roberto No, no puedo jugar porque estoy enfermo.

Melisa Lo siento. ¿Vas a jugar el jueves o el viernes?

Roberto Creo que sí. Voy a jugar el viernes.

Melisa Bueno. Llámame el viernes. Que te mejores.

Activity A

Choose the correct answer for each question.

1 When is Melisa going to play tennis?

   a today　　　　　**b tomorrow**

2 Why doesn't Roberto play with Melisa?

   a He doesn't want to.　**b He can't.**

3 What other day is he going to play?

   a Thursday　　　　**b Friday**

4 Who is going to call on Friday?

   a Melisa　　　　　**b Roberto**

Activity B

On Friday, Roberto sends Melisa a text message. Read his message and Melisa's response, then answer the questions.

> Lo siento Melisa, no puedo jugar hoy. Todavía estoy enfermo. ¿Vamos a jugar el domingo o el lunes? Roberto

> ¡Qué lástima! Pero, no te preocupes. Llámame el domingo. Melisa

1 Why can't Roberto play on Friday?

   a He's still sick.　　**b He doesn't want to.**

2 What does Melisa tell Roberto?

   a not to call her　　**b not to worry**

3 When will they talk again?

   a Sunday　　　　　**b Monday**

Activity C

Today is Sunday. Write a text message from Roberto to Melisa to tell her that he wants to play on Monday.

LESSON 2

Words to Know

Core Words

Los deportes (Sports)

el béisbol	baseball
el ciclismo	cycling
el fútbol	soccer
la natación	swimming
el tenis	tennis

La salud (Health)

delgado/delgada	slender (m/f)
enfermo/enferma	sick (m/f)
el estrés	stress
el gimnasio	gym
gordo/gorda	fat (m/f)
sano/sana	healthy (m/f)
el peso	weight
pesar	to weigh

Activity A

Write the name of the sport under each picture.

1 _____

2 _____

3 _____

4 _____

Activity B

Fill in the blanks with the correct Spanish word.

1   ¿Dónde está _____?
    the gym

2   ¿Cuál es su _____?
    weight

3   Él no quiere estar _____.
    fat

4   Ella come bien para estar _____
    slender

    y _____.
    healthy

5   ¿Por qué tiene _____?
    stress

6   ¿Está _____ Roberto?
    sick

Activity C

Match the English word to the correct Spanish translation.

1   slender

    a   el estrés   **b   delgado**

2   soccer

    a   el fútbol   **b   el béisbol**

3   to weigh

    a   pesar   **b   el peso**

4   healthy

    a   enfermo   **b   sano**

SMART TIP

There is also a feminine form of the word *gimnasio*; however, the two forms have different meanings. *Gimnasia* (f) refers to gymnastics and *gimnasio* (m) is a gym. Examples: *Voy al gimnasio* (I'm going to the gym). *Ana compite en gimnasia* (Ana competes in gymnastics).

Smart Phrases

Activity B

Choose the best phrase for each picture.

1

a Estoy enfermo.

b Estoy sano.

Core Phrases

¿Cómo se siente?	How are you feeling?
Estoy enfermo/enferma.	I'm sick. (m/f)
Estoy sano/sana.	I'm healthy. (m/f)
Quiero estar en forma.	I want to be in shape.
Quiero bajar de peso.	I want to lose weight.
Quiero subir de peso.	I want to gain weight.

2

a Quiero estar en forma.

b Estoy enferma.

Extra Phrases

Creo que sí.	I think so.
Lo siento.	I'm sorry.
¡Qué lástima!	What a shame!
Que te mejores.	Feel better.
todavía	still

3

a Quiero subir de peso.

b Estoy sana.

Activity A

What do you say if you want to…

1 …say you're healthy?

_____

2 …say you want to be in shape?

_____

3 …ask how someone is feeling?

_____

4 …say you want to lose weight?

_____

4

a Quiero subir de peso.

b Quiero bajar de peso.

5

a Estoy sano.

b Quiero bajar de peso.

Your Turn

¿Cómo se siente? Now talk about how you feel. Use *Me siento bien/mal* to tell if you feel well or bad. Then tell if you are *enfermo/enferma* or *sano/sana*. ¿Quiere subir o bajar de peso?

_____

_____

_____

LESSON 4

Smart Grammar

The future tense using *ir*

In Unit 9 you learned to use the future tense. You can also talk about the future using *ir* + *a* + infinitive verb.

Examples

Voy a jugar tenis.	I'm going to play tennis.
Vas a ver a la dentista.	You're going to see the dentist.
Vamos a vivir en España.	We're going to live in Spain.
Van a hablar con el profesor.	They're going to talk to the teacher.

Activity A

Write what each person is going to do. The personal pronoun and verb are provided for you.

1 él, escribir _____

2 yo, bailar _____

3 ellos, estudiar _____

4 nosotros, jugar _____

5 tú, cocinar _____

6 ella, correr _____

> **SMART TIP**
>
> The future tense with *–ir* is often used to talk about a plan. This form is more common than the simple future. For example, you will hear *Voy a jugar tenis la próxima semana* instead of *Jugaré tenis la próxima semana.*

Activity B

Make each sentence a question. The first one is done for you.

1 Voy a ver la película el viernes.

   ¿Cuándo vas a ver la película?

2 Va a llamar esta tarde.

   _____

3 Vamos a vivir en México.

   _____

4 Fabián va a llamar.

   _____

5 Emilia y Ernesto van a tomar cerveza.

   _____

6 Tú vas a limpiar los cuartos.

   _____

Your Turn

Look at each picture and tell what is going to happen.

  _____

_____

_____

 _____

_____

_____

  _____

_____

_____

 _____

_____

_____

LESSON 5
La medicina

Medical Advertisement
Read the advertisement; remember to look for cognates and root words you know for help.

Medicina para el resfriado

Ayuda con la fiebre y la tos.

Alivia el dolor de cabeza y garganta.

Esta medicina ayuda a que el cuerpo se sienta mejor.

¡Usted no necesita ir al doctor!

¡No necesita una receta!

alivia	alleviates
el cuerpo	the body

Activity A
Choose the correct answer for each question.

1 What is this ad for?

   a cold medicine   **b pain medicine**

2 What does the medicine help with?

   a fever   **b broken foot**

3 What does the medicine alleviate?

   a toothaches   **b headaches**

4 Why don't you need to see a doctor to get this medicine?

   a You don't need a prescription.   **b You don't need a shot.**

Read the advertisement; remember to look for cognates and root words you know for help.

Medicina para la tos

Ayuda con el dolor de garganta.

Alivia la fiebre y el dolor de cabeza.

Tome esta medicina dos veces a la semana.

¡Se va a sentir mejor con esta medicina!

Necesita una receta.

Activity B
Choose the correct answer for each question.

1 What is this ad for?

   a stomach medicine b cough medicine

2 What does the medicine help with?

   a headaches   **b sore throat**

3 What does the medicine alleviate?

   a fever   **b toothache**

4 How often should you take this medicine?

   a every day   **b twice a week**

5 Do you need to see a doctor to get this medicine?

   a yes   **b no**

Activity C
Complete the following sentences to compare both medicines.

La medicina para el resfriado ayuda _____ y la medicina _____ ayuda _____. Las dos medicinas alivian _____. La medicina de la tos alivia _____ y la medicina del resfriado alivia _____.

> ### CULTURE TIP
> Home remedies are often used to treat common ailments in Latin America. For example, a common *jarabe* (cough syrup) is made from combining anise, chamomile, cloves, lemon and honey. *Té de manzanilla* (chamomile tea) calms an upset stomach. *Limón con miel* (lemon with honey) soothes a sore throat.

Words to Know

Core Words

el dolor de cabeza	headache
el dolor de estómago	stomachache
el dolor de garganta	sore throat
el dolor de muela	toothache
la fiebre	fever
el resfriado	cold
la tos	cough
el dentista/la dentista	dentist (m/f)
el doctor/la doctora	doctor (m/f)
el hospital	hospital
la inyección	shot
la medicina	medicine
la receta	prescription

Activity A

You have various ailments. Circle the word that best completes the sentence.

1   Tienes tos. Necesitas _____.

   a un dentista   **b medicina**

2   Tienes dolor de muela. Vas al _____.

   a hospital   **b dentista**

3   Tienes fiebre. El doctor te va a dar una _____ para la medicina.

   a inyección   **b receta**

SMART TIP

When you say you have an ailment, you don't need to use an article before the noun. Examples:

Tengo dolor de cabeza.   I have a headache.
Tengo fiebre.   I have a fever.
Tengo tos.   I have a cough.

Activity B

The following people are not feeling well. Look at the pictures and write the corresponding ailments.

1 _____

2 _____

3 _____

4 _____

Your Turn

Usted es un doctor/una doctora. Talk about your patient. ¿Qué tiene el paciente? ¿Qué necesita?

_____

_____

_____

_____

CULTURE TIP

When looking for a pharmacy in Spain, look for the lit up green cross indicating an open pharmacy. Pharmacists in Spain are expected to give *consejo farmacéutico* (pharmaceutical advice) as part of their job and are there to help you. If you have any questions before going to a doctor, you can head to a pharmacist for medical advice.

Smart Phrases

Core Phrases

¿Qué le duele?	What hurts?
Me duele el brazo.	My arm hurts.
Me duele la espalda.	My back hurts.
Me duele la mano.	My hand hurts.
Me duelen los pies.	My feet hurt.
Me duelen las piernas.	My legs hurt.

Extra Phrases

¿Puede recomendarme un doctor/dentista?	Can you recommend a doctor/dentist?
Tiene que ver al doctor/dentista.	You need to see a doctor/dentist.

SMART TIPS

- The verb *doler* is reflexive. It has only two conjugations: *duele* and *duelen*. Use *duele* when talking about one part of the body that hurts and *duelen* when talking about two or more. For example:

  Me duele el pie.   My foot hurts.

  Me duelen los pies.   My feet hurt.

- *Me duele el brazo* literally means "the arm hurts me." To say "his/her arm hurts," say *Le duele el brazo* (literally, the arm hurts him or the arm hurts her).

Activity A

Look at each picture and complete each sentence.

1.   Me duele _____

2.   Le duele _____

3.   Me duelen _____

4.   Le duele _____

Activity B

You are waiting to see the doctor. Tell the *enfermera* (nurse, f) how you feel. Then tell her your symptoms.

Choose words or phrases from the box to write your description.

enfermo	brazo	me duele la espalda
fiebre	me duele el brazo	cabeza

_____

_____

_____

_____

_____

Activity C

Write *el reporte de la enfermera* (the nurse's report) based on what you told her in Activity B. Use *le* instead of *me*.

_____

_____

_____

LESSON 8

Smart Grammar

Adverbs of Time

Use the following words when talking about how frequently something happens.

a menudo	often
a veces	sometimes
nunca	never
siempre	always
una vez/dos veces	once/twice
usualmente	usually
todos los días	every day

Examples

Juego béisbol a menudo.	I play baseball often.
Usualmente Roberto está en forma.	Roberto is usually in shape.
Nunca hago gimnasia.	I never do gymnastics.
Hago ejercicio todos los días.	I exercise every day.

Activity A

Choose the word that best describes how often you do these activities or how often this happens to you.

1 Me enfermo.
   a a menudo   **b a veces**   **c nunca**

2 Hago ejercicio.
   a a menudo   **b a veces**   **c nunca**

3 Juego tenis dos veces a la semana.
   a a menudo   **b a veces**   **c nunca**

4 Hago gimnasia los domingos.
   a a menudo   **b a veces**   **c nunca**

Activity B

Translate these sentences from English to Spanish.

1 I sometimes play tennis.

   _____

2 I always go to the gym.

   _____

3 I am usually healthy.

   _____

4 I play tennis once a week.

   _____

5 I never take medicine.

   _____

6 I run every day.

   _____

Activity C

Now translate these questions.

1 Do you always go to Cartagena in July?

   _____

2 Do you usually travel during the summer?

   _____

3 Does Esteban eat lunch at home every day?

   _____

Your Turn

In Spanish, tell what you do or don't do in these time frames.

1 cada mes _____

2 a veces _____

3 nunca _____

4 siempre _____

Activity A

Los hermanos Carlos y Carlota don't agree on anything. Carlos will say something and Carlota will immediately say the opposite or something else. Fill in Carlota's half of the dialogue with the appropriate Spanish phrases.

Carlos Me siento mal.

Carlota _____
I feel good.

Carlos Estoy enfermo.

Carlota _____
I'm healthy.

Carlos Voy a ver a la dentista.

Carlota _____
I'm not going to see the dentist.

Carlos Tengo dolor de cabeza.

Carlota _____
I have a stomachache.

Carlos Quiero ir al doctor.

Carlota _____
I don't want to go to the doctor.

Carlos Hago ejercicio porque quiero estar en forma.

Carlota _____
I exercise because I want to lose weight.

Activity B

What's wrong with these sentences? Rewrite them so that they are grammatically correct.

1 Me duelen la cabeza. _____

2 Voy vivir en Perú. _____

3 Hago ejercicio dos vez a la semana.
_____

4 Teresa van a correr en el parque.
_____

5 Vas a cocinas la cena. _____

6 Me duele los pies. _____

Activity C

Use the pictures as clues to unscramble the anagrams. You will create words you learned in this unit.

1 i l c o m s i c   _ _ _ _ _ _ _ _

2 s e n t i   _ _ _ _ _

3 m e r o f e n   _ _ _ _ _ _ _

4 a n i i c d e m   _ _ _ _ _ _ _ _

5 b r i e f e   _ _ _ _ _ _

6 a s t i t e n d   _ _ _ _ _ _ _ _

Challenge

Answer the following questions based on your life.

¿Qué va a cocinar mañana? _____

¿Qué hace a menudo para divertirse? _____

¿Qué va a hacer el próximo mes? _____

Internet Activity

Go to **www.berlitzbooks.com/5minute** for a list of websites for gyms in Spain and Latin American countries. Select a gym, then find out what the gym offers. What kinds of memberships are available? What are the facilities like? Are there exercise classes?

A

el abrigo	ehl ah·bree·goh	coat
abril	ah·breel	April
la abuela	lah ah·bweh·lah	grandmother
el abuelo	ehl ah·bweh·loh	grandfather
el aeropuerto	ehl ah·eh·roh·pwehr·toh	airport
agosto	ah·gohs·toh	August
el agua	ehl ah·gwah	water
alemán	ah·leh·mahn	German m
alemana	ah·leh·mah·nah	German f
Alemania	ah·leh·mah·neeyah	Germany
amarillo	ah·mah·reeyoh	yellow
anoche	ah·noh·cheh	last night adv
anteayer	ahn·teh·ah·yehr	the day before adv
el apartamento	ehl ah·pahr·tah·mehn·toh	apartment, flat BE
el armario	ehl ahr·mah·reeyoh	closet
el arroz	ehl ah·rrohs	rice
el asistente	ehl ah·see·stehn·teh	assistant
la asistente	lah ah·see·stehn·teh	assistant
atrás de	ah·trahs deh	behind
Australia	awh·strah·leeyah	Australia
australiana	awh·strah·leeyah·nah	Australian f
australiano	awh·strah·leeyah·no	Australian m
el autobús	ehl awhtoh·boos	bus
la avenida	lah ah·behn·ee·dah	avenue
el avión	ehl ah·beeyohn	airplane, plane aeroplane BE
ayer	ah·yehr	yesterday adv
azul	ah·sool	blue

B

bailar	bayee·lahr	dance v
el baño	ehl bah·nyoh	bathroom
el bar	ehl bahr	bar, pub BE
beber	beh·behr	drink v
las bebidas	lahs beh·bee·dahs	drinks
el béisbol	ehl beyees·bohl	baseball
la biblioteca	lah bee·bleeyoh·teh·kah	library

blanco	blahn·koh	white
la blusa	lah bloo·sah	blouse
el boleto	ehl boh·leh·toh	ticket
las botas	lahs boh·tahs	boots

C

el café	ehl kah·feh	coffee
cálido	kah·lee·doh	warm (temperature)
la calle	lah kah·yeh	street
calor	kah·lohr	hot, warm (temperature)
la camisa	lah kah·mee·sah	shirt
la camiseta	lah kah·mee·seh·tah	T-shirt
Canadá	kah·nah·dah	Canada
canadiense	kah·nah·deeyen·seh	Canadian
la carne	lah kahr·neh	meat
el carro	ehl kah·rroh	car
la casa	lah kah·sah	house
catorce	kah·tohr·seh	14
cerca de	sehr·kah deh	near
la cerveza	lah sehr·beh·sah	beer
la chaqueta	lah chah·keh·tah	jacket
el cheque	ehl cheh·keh	check n, cheque BE
el ciclismo	ehl see·klees·moh	cycling
cinco	seen·koh	5
cincuenta	seen·kwehn·tah	50
el cine	ehl see·neh	movie theater, cinema BE
el clima	ehl klee·mah	weather
la cocina	lah koh·see·nah	kitchen
los colores	lohs koh·lohr·ehs	colors
el comedor	ehl koh·meh·dohr	dining room
comer	koh·mehr	eat v
la comida	lah koh·mee·dah	food
el concierto	ehl kohn·see·ehr·toh	concert
la corbata	lah kohr·bah·tah	tie (clothing)
cuarenta	kwah·rehn·tah	40
los cuartos	lohs kwahr·tohs	rooms
cuatro	kwah·troh	4

---

adj	adjective	BE	British English	v	verb	adv	adverb	n	noun

D

datos personales	dah·tohs per·sohn·ah·lehs	personal information
delante de	deh·lahn·teh deh	in front of
delgada	dehl·gah·dah	slender f
delgado	dehl·gah·doh	slender m
el dentista	ehl dehn·tee·stah	dentist m
la dentista	lah dehn·tee·stah	dentist f
los deportes	lohs deh·pohr·tehs	sports
a la derecha	ah lah deh·reh·chah	to the right
el día	ehl deeyah	day
los días de	lohs deeyas deh	days of the week
la semana	lah seh·mah·na	
diciembre	dee·seeyehm·breh	December
diecinueve	deeyeh·see·nweh·beh	19
dieciocho	deeyeh·see·oh·choh	18
dieciséis	deeyeh·see·seyees	16
diecisiete	deeyeh·see·seeyeh·teh	17
diez	deeyehs	10
el dinero	ehl dee·neh·roh	money
la dirección	lah dee·rehk·seeyohn	address
doce	doh·seh	12
el doctor	ehl dohk·tohr	doctor m
la doctora	lah dohk·toh·rah	doctor f
el dólar	ehl doh·lahr	dollar (U.S.)
el dolor	ehl doh·lohr	pain
el dolor	ehl doh·lohr	headache
de cabeza	deh kah·beh·sah	
el dolor	ehl doh·lohr	stomachache
de estómago	deh eh·stoh·mah·goh	
el dolor	ehl doh·lohr	sore throat
de garganta	deh gahr·gahn·tah	
el dolor	ehl doh·lohr	toothache
de muela	deh mweh·lah	
el domingo	ehl doh·meen·goh	Sunday
el dormitorio	ehl dohr·mee·toh·reeyoh	bedroom
dos	dohs	2

E

el edificio	ehl eh·dee·fee·seeyoh	building
el efectivo	ehl eh·fehk·tee·boh	cash
la empleada	lah ehm·pleh·ah·dah	employee f
el empleado	ehl ehm·pleh·ah·doh	employee m
enero	eh·neh·roh	January
enferma	ehn·fehr·mah	sick f
enfermo	ehn·fehr·moh	sick m
la ensalada	lah ehn·sah·lah·dah	salad
el equipaje	ehl eh·kee·pah·kheh	luggage, baggage BE
la escuela	lah ehs·kweh·lah	school
España	eh·spah·nyah	Spain
español	ehs·pah·nyohl	Spanish m
española	ehs·pah·nyoh·lah	Spanish f
la esposa	lah ehs·poh·sah	wife
el esposo	ehl ehs·poh·soh	husband
la estación	lah eh·stah·seeyohn	station
la estación	lah eh·stah·seeyohn	subway, underground BE
de metro	deh meh·troh	
la estación	lah eh·stah·seeyohn	train station
de tren	deh trehn	
los estaciones	lohs eh·stah·seeyohn·ehs	seasons
los Estados	lohs ehs·tah·dohs	United States
Unidos	oo·nee·dohs	
estadounidense	eh·stah·doh·oo·nee·dehn·seh	American
el estrés	ehl eh·strehs	stress
el estudiante	ehl eh·stoo·deeyahn·teh	student m
la estudiante	lah eh·stoo·deeyahn·teh	student f
extra grande	ehks·trah grahn·deh	extra large

F

la falda	lah fahl·dah	skirt
la familia	lah fah·mee·leeyah	family
febrero	feh·breh·roh	February
la fiebre	lah feeyeh·breh	fever, temperature BE
francés	frahn·sehs	French m
francesa	frahn·seh·sah	French f

adj adjective	BE British English	v verb	adv adverb	n noun

Francia	frahn·seeyah	France
frío	free·oh	cold, cool (temperature)
la fruta	lah froo·tah	fruit
el fútbol	ehl foot·bohl	soccer, football BE

G

el gato	ehl gah·toh	cat
el gimnasio	ehl kheem·nah·see·oh	gym
gordo/gorda	gohr·doh/gohr·dah	fat m/f
grande	grahn·deh	large
los guantes	lohs gwahn·tehs	gloves

H

el helado	ehl ehl·ah·doh	frozen adj ice cream n
la hermana	lah ehr·mah·nah	sister
el hermano	ehl ehr·mah·noh	brother
los hermanos	lohs ehr·mah·nohs	siblings
la hija	lah ee·khah	daughter
el hijo	ehl ee·khoh	son
el hombre	ehl ohm·breh	man
la hora	lah oh·rah	hour
el hospital	ehl oh·spee·tahl	hospital
húmedo	oo·meh·doh	humid

I

la iglesia	lah ee·gleh·seeyah	church
el impuesto sobre ventas	ehl eem·pweh·stoh soh·breh behn·tahs	sales tax
inglés/inglesa	een·glehs/een·gleh·sah	English m/f
el invierno	ehl een·beeyehr·noh	winter
la inyección	lah een·yehk·seeyohn	injection, shot
Irlanda	eer·lahn·dah	Ireland
irlandés	eer·lahn·dehs	Irish m

irlandesa	eer·lahn·deh·sah	Irish f
Italia	ee·tah·leeyah	Italy
italiana	ee·tah·leeyah·nah	Italian f
italiano	ee·tah·leeyah·noh	Italian m
a la izquierda	ah lah ees·keeyehr·dah	to the left

J

el jefe/la jefa	ehl kheh·feh/lah kheh·fah	employer
el jueves	ehl khweh·behs	Thursday
el jugo	ehl khoo·goh	juice
julio	khoo·leeyoh	July
junio	khoo·neeyoh	June

L

la leche	lah leh·cheh	milk
lejos de	leh·khohs deh	far from
el lunes	ehl loo·nehs	Monday
lluvioso	yoo·beeyoh·soh	rainy

M

la madre	lah mah·dreh	mother
la maleta	lah mah·leh·tah	bag, suitcase
el martes	ehl mahr·tehs	Tuesday
marzo	mahr·soh	March
mayo	mah·yoh	May
mediana	meh·deeyah·nah	medium
la medicina	lah meh·dee·see·nah	medicine
el mes	ehl mehs	month
los meses del año	lohs meh·sehs dehl ah·nyoh	months of the year
México	meh·khee·koh	Mexico
mexicana	meh·khee·kah·nah	Mexican f
mexicano	meh·khee·kah·noh	Mexican m
el miércoles	ehl meeyehr·koh·lehs	Wednesday
el minuto	ehl mee·noo·toh	minute

adj adjective	BE British English	v verb	adv adverb	n noun

| morado | moh·rah·doh | purple |
| la mujer | lah moo·khehr | woman |

N

la natación	lah nah·tah·see·ohn	swimming
negro	neh·groh	black
la nieta	lah neeyeh·tah	granddaughter
el nieto	ehl neeyeh·toh	grandson
la niña	lah nee·nyah	girl
el niño	ehl nee·nyoh	boy
noviembre	noh·beeyehm·breh	November
nublado	noo·blah·doh	snowy
nueve	nweh·beh	9
el número	ehl noo·meh·roh	number

O

ocho	oh·choh	8
octubre	ohk·too·breh	October
la oficina de correos	lah oh·fee·see·nah deh coh·rreyohs	post office
once	ohn·seh	11
el otoño	ehl oh·toh·nyoh	autumn, fall

P

el padre	ehl pah·dreh	father
los padres	lohs pah·drehs	parents
el pájaro	ehl pah·khah·roh	bird
el pan	ehl pahn	bread
los pantalones	lohs pahn·tah·loh·nes	pants, trousers BE
las papas	lahs pah·pas	potatoes
la parada de autobús	lah pah·rah·dah deh awhtoh·boos	bus stop
el pasaporte	ehl pah·sah·pohr·teh	passport
el pastel	ehl pahs·tehl	cake

la película	lah peh·lee·koo·lah	movie
pequeña	peh·keh·nyah	small
el periódico	ehl peh·reeyoh·dee·koh	newspaper
el periodista	ehl peh·reeyoh·dee·stah	journalist m
la periodista	lah peh·reeyoh·dee·stah	journalist f
el perro	ehl peh·rroh	dog
Perú	peh·roo	Peru
peruana	peh·roo·ah·nah	Peruvian f
peruano	peh·roo·ah·noh	Peruvian m
pesar	peh·sahr	weigh v
el pescado	ehl pehs·kah·doh	fish
el peso	ehl peh·soh	weight
el pollo	ehl poh·yoh	chicken
Portugal	pohr·too·gahl	Portugal
portugués	pohr·too·ghehs	Portuguese m
portuguesa	pohr·too·gheh·sah	Portuguese f
la prima	lah pree·mah	cousin f
la primavera	lah pree·mah·beh·rah	spring
el primo	ehl pree·moh	cousin m
la profesión	lah proh·feh·seeyohn	job, profession
el profesor	ehl proh·feh·sohr	teacher m
la profesora	lah proh·feh·soh·rah	teacher f
en punto	ehn poon·toh	o'clock

Q

| el queso | ehl keh·soh | cheese |
| quince | keen·seh | 15 |

R

la receta	lah reh·seh·tah	prescription
el recibo	ehl reh·see·boh	receipt
el Reino Unido	ehl reyee·noh oo·nee·doh	United Kingdom (U.K.)
el resfriado	ehl rehs·free·ah·doh	cold (health)
la revista	lah reh·bee·stah	magazine
rojo	roh·khoh	red
rosa	roh·sah	pink

| adj | adjective | BE | British English | v | verb | adv | adverb | n | noun |

S

el sábado	ehl sah·bah·doh	Saturday
la sala	lah sah·lah	living room
el salón	ehl sah·lohn	classroom
las sandalias	las sahn·dah·leeyahs	sandals
sano/sana	sah·noh/sah·nah	healthy m/f
la secretaria	lah seh·kreh·tah·reeyah	secretary f
el secretario	ehl seh·kreh·tah·reeyoh	secretary m
el segundo	ehl seh·goon·doh	second
seis	seyees	6
la semana pasada	lah seh·mah·nah pah·sah·dah	last week adv
septiembre	sehp·teeyehm·breh	September
sesenta	seh·sehn·tah	60
siete	seeyeh·teh	7
la sobrina	lah soh·bree·nah	niece
el sobrino	ehl soh·bree·noh	nephew
soleado	soh·leh·ah·doh	sunny
el sombrero	ehl sohm·breh·roh	hat
la sopa	lah soh·pah	soup
el sueldo	ehl swehl·doh	salary, wage
el supermercado	ehl soo·pehr·mehr·kah·doh	grocery store, supermarket

T

las tallas	lahs tah·yahs	sizes
la tarjeta de crédito	lah tahr·kheh·tah deh kreh·dee·toh	credit card
la tarjeta de débito	lah tahr·kheh·tah deh deh·bee·toh	debit card
el teatro	ehl teh·ah·troh	theater
el té	ehl teh	tea
el teléfono	ehl teh·leh·foh·noh	telephone
el tenis	ehl teh·nees	tennis
la tía	lah teeyah	aunt
el tío	ehl teeyoh	uncle

tomar	toh·mahr	take v
la tos	lah tohs	cough n
el trabajo	ehl trah·bah·khoh	work n
trece	treh·seh	13
treinta	treyeen·tah	30
treinta y cinco	treyeen·tah ee seen·koh	35
treinta y cuatro	treyeen·tah ee kwah·troh	34
treinta y dos	treyeen·tah ee dohs	32
treinta y tres	treyeen·tah ee trehs	33
treinta y uno	treyeen·tah ee oo·noh	31
tres	trehs	3

U

uno	oo·noh	1

V

las vacaciones	lahs bah·kah·seeyohn·ehs	vacation, holiday BE
los vegetales	lohs beh·kheh·tah·lehs	vegetables
veinte	beyeen·teh	20
el verano	ehl beh·rah·noh	summer
verde	behr·deh	green
el vestido	ehl behs·tee·doh	dress (piece of clothing)
el viaje	ehl beeyah·kheh	trip
con viento	kohn beeyehn·toh	windy
el viernes	ehl beeyehr·nehs	Friday
el vuelo	ehl bweh·loh	flight

adj adjective	BE British English	v verb	adv adverb	n noun

Numbers

los números	lohs noo·meh·rohs	
uno	oo·noh	1
dos	dohs	2
tres	trehs	3
cuatro	kwah·troh	4
cinco	seen·koh	5
seis	seyees	6
siete	seeyeh·teh	7
ocho	oh·choh	8
nueve	nweh·beh	9
diez	deeyehs	10
once	ohn·seh	11
doce	doh·seh	12
trece	treh·seh	13
catorce	kah·tohr·seh	14
quince	keen·seh	15
dieciséis	deeyeh·see·seyees	16
diecisiete	deeyeh·see·seeyeh·teh	17
dieciocho	deeyeh·see·oh·choh	18
diecinueve	deeyeh·see·nweh·beh	19
veinte	beyeen·teh	20
treinta	treyeen·tah	30
treinta y uno	treyeen·tah ee oo·noh	31
treinta y dos	treyeen·tah ee dohs	32
treinta y tres	treyeen·tah ee trehs	33
treinta y cuatro	treyeen·tah ee kwah·troh	34
treinta y cinco	treyeen·tah ee seen·koh	35
cuarenta	kwah·rehn·tah	40
cincuenta	seen·kwehn·tah	50
sesenta	seh·sehn·tah	60

Days

los días	lohs deeyas	
el lunes	ehl loo·nehs	Monday
el martes	ehl mahr·tehs	Tuesday
el miércoles	ehl meeyehr·koh·lehs	Wednesday
el jueves	ehl khweh·behs	Thursday
el viernes	ehl beeyehr·nehs	Friday
el sábado	ehl sah·bah·doh	Saturday
el domingo	ehl doh·meen·goh	Sunday

Months

los meses	lohs meh·sehs	
enero	eh·neh·roh	January
febrero	feh·breh·roh	February
marzo	mahr·soh	March
abril	ah·breel	April
mayo	mah·yoh	May
junio	khoo·neeyoh	June
julio	khoo·leeyoh	July
agosto	ah·gohs·toh	August
septiembre	sehp·teeyehm·breh	September
octubre	ohk·too·breh	October
noviembre	noh·beeyehm·breh	November
diciembre	dee·seeyehm·breh	December

Colors

los colores   lohs koh·lohr·ehs   colours BE

amarillo
ah·mah·<u>reeyoh</u>
yellow

azul
ah·<u>sool</u>
blue

blanco
<u>blahn</u>·koh
white

morado
moh·<u>rah</u>·doh
purple

negro
<u>neh</u>·groh
black

rojo
<u>roh</u>·khoh
red

rosa
<u>roh</u>·sah
rose

verde
<u>behr</u>·deh
green

Seasons

la primavera

lah pree·mah·<u>beh</u>·rah

spring

el invierno

ehl een·<u>beeyehr</u>·noh

winter

el verano

ehl beh·<u>rah</u>·noh

summer

el otoño

ehl oh·<u>toh</u>·nyoh

autumn, fall

adj adjective   BE British English   v verb   adv adverb   n noun

Countries/Nationalities

Alemania	ah·leh·<u>mah</u>·neeyah	Germany
alemán	ah·leh·<u>mahn</u>	German m
alemana	ah·leh·<u>mah</u>·nah	German f

Australia	awh·<u>strah</u>·leeyah	Australia
australiano	awh·strah·<u>leeyah</u>·no	Australian m
australiana	awh·strah·<u>leeyah</u>·nah	Australian f

Canadá	kah·nah·<u>dah</u>	Canada
canadiense	kah·nah·<u>deeyen</u>·seh	Canadian

España	eh·<u>spah</u>·nyah	Spain
español	ehs·pah·<u>nyohl</u>	Spanish m
española	ehs·pah·<u>nyoh</u>·lah	Spanish f

los Estados Unidos	lohs ehs·<u>tah</u>·dohs oo·<u>nee</u>·dohs	United States
estadounidense	eh·stah·doh·oo·nee·<u>dehn</u>·seh	American

Francia	<u>frahn</u>·seeyah	France
francés	frahn·<u>sehs</u>	French m
francesa	frahn·<u>seh</u>·sah	French f

Irlanda	eer·<u>lahn</u>·dah	Ireland
irlandés	eer·lahn·<u>dehs</u>	Irish m
irlandesa	eer·lahn·<u>deh</u>·sah	Irish f

Italia	ee·<u>tah</u>·leeyah	Italy
italiano	ee·tah·<u>leeyah</u>·noh	Italian m
italiana	ee·tah·<u>leeyah</u>·nah	Italian f

México	<u>meh</u>·khee·koh	Mexico
mexicano	meh·khee·<u>kah</u>·noh	Mexican m
mexicana	meh·khee·<u>kah</u>·nah	Mexican f

Perú	peh·<u>roo</u>	Peru
peruano	peh·roo·<u>ah</u>·noh	Peruvian m
peruana	peh·roo·<u>ah</u>·nah	Peruvian f

Portugal	pohr·too·<u>gahl</u>	Portugal
portugués	pohr·too·<u>ghehs</u>	Portuguese m
portuguesa	pohr·too·<u>gheh</u>·sah	Portuguese f

el Reino Unido	ehl <u>reyee</u>·noh oo·<u>nee</u>·doh	United Kingdom
inglés	een·<u>glehs</u>	English m
inglesa	een·<u>gleh</u>·sah	English f

adj adjective	BE British English	v verb	adv adverb	n noun

Extra Words

el artículo	ehl ahr·tee·koo·loh	article
la billetera	lah bee·yeh·teh·rah	wallet
el cambio	ehl kahm·bee·yoh	change (money)
los centavos	lohs sehn·tah·bohs	cents
la compañía	lah kohm·pah·nyeeyah	company
la cuadra	lah kwah·drah	block
el cuarto	ehl kwahr·toh	quarter
la cuñada	lah koo·nyah·dah	sister-in-law
el cuñado	ehl koo·nyah·doh	brother-in-law
dificil	dee·fee·seel	difficult
el empleador	ehl ehm·plee·ah·dohr	employer
los escaleras	lohs ehs·kah·leh·rahs	stairs
la esquina	lah ehs·kee·nah	corner
facil	fah·seel	easy
el hotel	ehl oh·tehl	hotel
el jardín	ehl khahr·deen	garden
el mayor	ehl mah·yohr	oldest
la media	lah meh·dee·yah	half
el menor	ehl meh·nohr	youngest
la moneda	lah moh·neh·dah	coin
mucho	moo·choh	a lot
nadar	nah·dahr	swim v
el negocio	ehl neh·goh·seeyoh	businees
la nuera	lah nweh·rah	daughter-in-law
la parada	lah pah·rah·dah	layover, stop BE
la reservación	lah reh·sehr·bah·seeyohn	reservation
la suegra	lah sweh·grah	mother-in-law
el suegro	ehl sweh·groh	father-in-law
el suelo	ehl sweh·loh	floor
usar	oo·sahr	wear v, use v
la ventana	lah vehn·tah·nah	window
viajar	beeyah·khar	travel v
el yerno	ehl yehr·noh	son-in-law

adj adjective	BE British English	v verb	adv adverb	n noun

Unit 1 Lesson 1

Activity A

1 T; 2 T; 3 F; 4 T

Activity B

Me llamo Lisa. ¿Cómo se llama usted?; Me llamo Marco. Mucho gusto.; Soy de España. Y usted, ¿de dónde es?; Soy de México.

Lesson 2

Activity A

1 ¡Hola!; 2 ¿Cómo se llama usted?; 3 ¿De dónde es?; 4 ¡Adiós!/Hasta luego.

Activity B

1 Buenas tardes.; 2 Buenas noches.; 3 Buenos días.

Lesson 3

Activity A

América del Norte y del Sur, top to bottom: 6; 4; 3; 1
Europa, top to bottom: 2; 5

Activity B

From left to right: 4; 3; 1; 2

Lesson 4

Activity A

1 yo; 2 ella; 3 él; 4 tú

Activity B

1 ellas; 2 ellos; 3 nosotras; 4 nosotros

Activity C

1 yo; 2 ella; 3 él; 4 ellas; 5 ellos

Lesson 5

Activity A

idioma; nacionalidad; español; inglés

Activity B

1 a; 2 b; 3 b; 4 b

Lesson 6

Activity A

1 mexicana; 2 estadounidense; 3 inglés; 4 australiano

Activity B

1 española; 2 inglesa; 3 mexicana; 4 estadounidense;
5 canadiense

Lesson 7

Activity A

1 ¿Es usted español?; 2 Hablo bien.; 3 Un poco.

Your Turn

Answers may vary. Possible answers:
Q1 ¡Hola! Me llamo Félix. ¿Cómo se llama usted?
A1 Soy Victor, mucho gusto.
Q2 ¿De dónde es usted?
A2 Soy español.

Lesson 8

Activity A

1 soy; 2 es; 3 eres; 4 es

Activity B

1 son; 2 somos; 3 son; 4 son

Your Turn

es usted; soy; son; Soy; es

Review

Activity A

Nombre	País	Nacionalidad
Pepa	España	española
Pablo	México	mexicana
Cassandra	Canadá	canadiense
Brian	Los Estados Unidos	estadounidense
Katie	El Reino Unido	inglesa

Activity B

1 Tú eres estadounidense.; 2 Lisa es española.; 3 Usted es canadiense.; 4 Ernesto es méxicano.

Activity C

Guía   ¡Hola! ¡Bienvenido a México!
Kiko   ¡Hola! Soy Kiko Buxó. ¿Cómo se llama usted?
Guía   Me llamo Enrico. Mucho gusto.
Kiko   Encantado. ¿Es usted mexicano?
Guía   Sí. ¿De dónde es usted?
Kiko   Soy del Reino Unido. ¿Habla inglés?
Guía   Un poquito.
Kiko   Hablo inglés y español.
Guía   ¡Qué bien!
Kiko   Hasta luego, Enrico.
Guía   ¡Adiós!

Activity D

Challenge

Perú; peruano

Activity E

1 ¡Hola! Me llamo Laura.; 2 Nosotros somos de Canadá.;
3 Pepinot es de España. Pepinot es español.; 4 Manuel es de los Estados Unidos.; 5 Yo hablo inglés.; 6 Ana es mexicana.

Unit 2 Lesson 1

Activity A   1 F; 2 F; 3 T; 4 T

Activity B

1 personas: niños; niñas; hombres; mujeres
2 cosas: casas; edificios; carros; autobuses
3 animales: gatos; perros; pájaros

Lesson 2

Activity A

1 a pájaro; b mujer; c hombre; d niño
2 a hombre; b autobús; c perro; d niño; e edificio; f gato; g mujer; h carro

Activity B

1 masculino; 2 masculino; 3 masculino; 4 femenino;
5 masculino; 6 femenino; 7 masculino; 8 masculino

Lesson 3

Activity A   1 ¡Mira a la gente!; 2 ¡Mira los animales!

Activity B

Querida Elena,
I'm having a great time here, and I'm learning some español.
¡Mira a la gente! There are hombres, mujeres y niños. ¡Mira las casas! ¡Mira el edificio! ¡Mira los animales! There are perros, gatos y pájaros.
Te extraño.

Lesson 4

Activity A   1 hombres; 2 bolsas; 3 lápices; 4 toros

Activity B   1 el; 2 la; 3 los; 4 las; 5 el; 6 el

Activity C   1 el gato; 2 las mujeres; 3 los carros; 4 la casa

Your Turn   1 la; 2 las; 3 el; 4 los; 5 la

Lesson 5

Activity A   1 c; 2 d; 3 b; 4 a

Activity B

Calle: Avenida Ricardo Palma; Número: 955;
Ciudad: Miraflores; Estado: Lima

Lesson 6

Activity A

dieciocho, diecinueve;
veinticuatro, veinticinco, veintiséis, veintisiete, veintiocho, veintinueve

Activity B

1 uno	4 cuatro
6 seis	9 nueve
13 trece	12 doce
18 dieciocho	15 quince
10 diez	22 veintidós
30 treinta	14 catorce

Activity C

1 14th Street; 2 27 Margarita Avenue;
3 Telephone: (178) 375-4219; 4 Zip Code: 11926

Lesson 7

Activity A

Answers may vary. Possible answers:
Me llamo _____.; Mi fecha de nacimiento es _____ _____.; Mi dirrección es _____; Mi número de teléfono es _____.

Activity B   1 a; 2 a; 3 a; 4 b

Lesson 8

Activity A

yo estudio; tú estudias; él/ella estudia; usted estudia; nosotros/nosotras estudiamos; ustedes estudian; ellos/ellas estudian

Activity B

yo vivo; tú vives; él/ella vive; usted vive; nosotros/nosotras vivimos; ustedes viven; ellos/ellas viven

Activity C

Tomás vive en Calle Orchard 10.; Julia y Max viven en Calle 7 10.; Carmen y yo vivimos en Calle Main 16.

Your Turn   Yo enseño inglés y español.; Marissa enseña inglés.

Review

Activity A

1 tres niños; 2 una casa; 3 dos teléfonos; 4 cinco mujeres

Activity B

1 Andrea vive en la Avenida 4, número 8.; 2 El número de teléfono de Javier es cuatro-ocho-dos nueve-uno-tres siete-tres-nueve-uno.; 3 Corrine y Mark viven en la Calle 4, número 30.; 4 El número de teléfono de Andrea es +44 20 2278 3625; 5 Javier vive en la Calle Huron 25.

Activity C

1 los pájaros; 2 las mujeres; 3 el autobús; 4 la dirección

Challenge

Answers may vary. Possible answers:
Él camina por Calle Main.; Ellos caminan por Calle Main.; Él sufre mucho.; Ellos sufren mucho.

Activity D

Laura ¡Hola! ¿Cómo se llama?
Usted ¡Hola! Me llamo (your name).
Laura Bien, ¿cuál es su número de teléfono?
Usted Mi número de teléfono es (your phone number).
Laura ¿Cuál es su dirrección?
Usted Mi dirección es (your address).
Laura ¿Y el código postal?
Usted Mi código postal es (your zip code).
Laura Por último, ¿cuál es su fecha de nacimiento?
Usted Mi fecha de nacimiento es (your date of birth).
Laura ¡Excelente! Bienvenido al Instituto de Idiomas Sancho.
Usted Muchas gracias.

Unit 3 Lesson 1

Activity A

1 Son las tres y treinta y cinco; 2 Faltan cincuenta y cinco minutos ; 3 Noventa minutos ; 4 Rayados

Activity B

1 ¿Qué hora es?; 2 Son las seis y treinta y cinco.; 3 ¡Es temprano! ¿Cuánto tiempo falta en el juego?; 4 Faltan cincuenta y cinco minutos.

Lesson 2

Activity A

1 Son las cuatro menos cuarto.; 2 Es la una y cuarto.; 3 Son las ocho y media.; 4 Son las doce.

Activity B

1 ¡Es temprano!; 2 ¡Es tarde!; 3 ¡Es temprano!; 4 ¡Es tarde!

Activity C

1 ¿Qué hora es?; 2 ¡Es temprano!; 3 ¡Es tarde!; 4 Son las dos de la mañana.

Lesson 3

Activity A

1 cuarenta y cuatro; 2 treinta y dos; 3 sesenta y siete; 4 cincuenta y ocho

Activity B

1 Faltan quince minutos. ; 2 Faltan seis horas y veintiocho minutos.; 3 Falta una hora y cuarenta y cinco minutos.; 4 Falta un minuto.

Your Turn

Son las cuatro y doce. Faltan treinta y tres minutos.; Son las cuatro y veintidos. Faltan veintitres minutos.; Son las cuatro y treinta y dos. Faltan trece minutos.; Son las cuatro y cuarenta y dos. Faltan tres minutos.

Lesson 4

Activity A

yo	corro
tú	corres
él/ella	corre
usted	corre
nosotros/nosotras	corremos
ustedes	corren
ellos/ellas	corren

Activity B

1 Yo veo; 2 Ella lee; 3 Nosotros comemos; 4 Ellas corren

Your Turn

Ellas comen un pastel y beben agua.

Lesson 5

Activity A

1 a ; 2 b; 3 a; 4 b; 5 b

Activity B

1 hacer los deberes; 2 llamar a Rosario; 3 lavar la ropa; 4 hacer ejercicio

Lesson 6

Activity A

1 martes; 2 lunes y jueves ; 3 viernes; 4 miércoles y sábado; 5 domingo

Activity B

1 lunes, 17 de noviembre; 2 sábado, 5 de junio; 3 miércoles, 21 de septiembre; 4 viernes, 8 de abril; 5 martes, 31 de enero; 6 domingo, 12 de agosto; 7 jueves, 25 de marzo; 8 domingo, 14 de octubre; 9 lunes, 29 de mayo; 10 martes, 2 de diciembre; 11 viernes, 15 de julio; 12 miércoles, 18 de febrero

Lesson 7

Activity A

1 b; 2 b; 3 a; 4 b

Activity B

1 ¿Qué día es hoy?; 2 ¿Cuál es la fecha de hoy?; 3 ¿En qué mes estamos?; 4 ¿En qué año estamos?

Lesson 8

Activity A

1 haces; 2 hace; 3 hacen; 4 hacemos

Activity B

1 c; 2 a; 3 b

Your Turn

Answers will vary but make sure to include *hago* in the answer; possible answers may be:
Hago ejercicio los sábados.
Hago mis deberes los domingos.

Review

Activity A

Activities may be in a different order than what you wrote.
2 Irene barre el suelo a las nueve menos cuarto de la noche.; 3 Irene llama a Pedro a las seis de la tarde.; 4 Irene hace ejercicio a las ocho menos cuarto de la mañana.; 5 Irene lava la ropa a las once y cuarto de la mañana.

Activity B

1 Faltan dos horas, treinta y cuatro minutos y trece segundos.; 2 Faltan veintisiete segundos.; 3 Faltan doce minutos y treinta y nueve segundos.

Activity C

1 domingo, veintiuno de febrero; 2 sábado, trece de febrero; 3 martes, veintitres de febrero; 4 lunes, quince de febrero

Unit 4 Lesson 1

Activity A

1 F; 2 T; 3 F; 4 F

Activity B

1 a; 2 a; 3 b; 4 b; 5 b

Lesson 2

Activity A

Somos cinco personas en mi familia. Tomás es mi padre. Mi madre se llama Mariana. Raquel es mi hermana. Pablo es el esposo de Raquel.

Activity B

1 hermanos; 2 hermano; 3 madre; 4 padre; 5 padres; 6 hijo; 7 hija; 8 hijos; 9 esposa; 10 esposo

Lesson 3

Activity A

1 ¿Qué tan grande es su familia?; 2 Somos ocho en la familia. Mire esta foto.; 3 ¡Qué familia tan grande!; 4 Sí, mi familia es grande. Y, ¿es grande su familia?; 5 No. Mi familia es pequeña. Somos cuatro personas.

Activity B

1 ¡Qué familia tan pequeña!; 2 ¡Qué familia tan grande!; 3 ¡Qué familia tan grande!; 4 ¡Qué familia tan pequeña!

Lesson 4

Activity A

1 mi; 2 tu; 3 Su; 4 mis; 5 tus; 6 sus; 7 Nuestra; 8 nuestros

Activity B

1 e; 2 b; 3 h; 4 d; 5 c; 6 g; 7 a; 8 f

Lesson 5

Activity A

1 su abuelo; 2 su madre; 3 su prima; 4 su sobrina

Activity B

1 el primo; 2 la prima; 3 la abuela; 4 el sobrino

Lesson 6

Activity A

1 prima; 2 sobrino; 3 tía; 4 nieto; 5 abuelo; 6 abuelos

Activity B

1 a; 2 a; 3 b; 4 a; 5 a; 6 b

Lesson 7

Activity A

1 Sí, mi familia es muy unida.; 2 No, es soltero.; 3 Sí, tengo una familia muy grande.; 4 No, soy casada. Ese es mi esposo.

Activity B

1 Te amo.; 2 Te quiero.; 3 Tengo una familia unida.; 4 ¿Eres casado/casada?

Lesson 8

Activity A

1 un abuelo; 2 unas niñas ; 3 una niña; 4 unos hombres

Activity B

Answers will vary. Possible answers: 1 Tú tienes un hermano.; 2 Yo tengo un primo.; 3 Ellos tienen dos tías.; 4 Ustedes tienen tres sobrinas.

Your Turn

Answers will vary. 1 Sí, tengo dos tíos/ No, no tengo tíos.; 2 Sí, tengo tres sobrinos/ No, no tengo sobrinos.; 3 Sí, mis tíos tienen hijos/ No, mis tíos no tienen hijos.; 4 Sí, mis primos tienen hijos/ No, mis primos no tienen hijos.

Review

Activity A

Gisela	Este es mi abuelo, Alfonso. Y esta es mi abuela, Ramona.
Carlos	¿Quién es esta mujer?
Gisela	Ella es mi prima, Pía y este es su hemano, Pepe.
Carlos	¿Esta es tu madre?
Gisela	No, esa es mi tía, Consuelo. Pía y Pepe son sus hijos.
Carlos	¿Esta es tu madre?
Gisela	No, esta es mi tía Linda, la esposa de mi tío José. Él es el hermano de mi padre.
Carlos	Tu familia es grande. Y, ¿dónde está tu madre?
Gisela	Mis padres no están en la fiesta.

Activity B

1 Ramona es su abuela; 2 Pía y Pepe son sus sobrinos; 3 Consuelo y Linda son sus tías; 4 José es su tío.

Activity C

Answers will vary. Possible answers:

Carlos	Mi familia es grande/ Mi familia es pequeña.
Carlos	Sí, tengo hermanos/ No, no tengo hermanos.
Carlos	Sí, tengo tíos/ No, no tengo tíos.

Activity D

Carlos	¿Es ese su nieto?
Alfonso	No, este es mi nieto.
Carlos	¿Quién es esa?
Alfonso	Esa es mi sobrina.
Carlos	¡Esas son sus hijas!
Alfonso	No, esas son mis primas.

Activity E

1 Ellos tienen dos hijos.; 2 Ellos tienen tres hijos.; 3 Ella tiene dos hijas.; 4 Él tiene un hijo.

Unit 5 Lesson 1

Activity A   1 T; 2 T; 3 F; 4 F

Activity B   1 a; 2 b; 3 b; 4 b

Lesson 2

Activity A   1 la fruta; 2 el café; 3 la sopa; 4 la cerveza

Activity B   1 Como pan y bebo café.; 2 Como fruta y bebo agua.; 3 Como sopa y bebo cerveza.

Lesson 3

Activity A   1 Tengo hambre.; 2 Tengo sed.; 3 Tengo hambre.; 4 Tengo sed.; 5 Tengo hambre.; 6 Tengo sed.

Activity B   1 Tengo ganas de comer ensalada.; 2 Tengo ganas de beber jugo.

Activity C   1 Vamos a desayunar.; 2 Vamos a almorzar.; 3 Vamos a cenar.

Lesson 4

Activity A   1 Dónde; 2 Cuál; 3 Quién; 4 Cuándo

Activity B   Possible answers: 1 ¿Cuáles son sus hermanas?; 2 ¿Cómo es su casa?; 3 ¿Por qué está triste?; 4 ¿Qué día es hoy?; 5 ¿Quiénes son los niños?

Activity C   1 Por qué; 2 Quién; 3 Cuándo; 4 Cuál; 5 Dónde

Your Turn   1 ¿Cómo se llama su madre?; 2 ¿Qué hora es?; 3 ¿Quiénes son ellos?; 4 ¿Quién es él?

Lesson 5

Activity A   1 b; 2 a; 3 a; 4 a

Activity B   1 ¿Qué quiere de aperitivo?; 2 De aperitivo, quiero una ensalada; 3 ¿Y de plato principal?; 4 Quiero el pollo.

Lesson 6

Activity A   1 aperitivo; 2 plato principal; 3 postre; 4 plato principal

Activity B   1 a; 2 b; 3 a; 4 Los vegetales vienen con el pescado.

Your Turn
Answers may vary.
Possible answers are:

Restaurante _____
Menú

Aperitivo
Ensalada
Plato principal
Carne con ensalada de papas
Postre
Ensalada de frutas
Helado de chocolate
Bebidas
Jugo
Agua
Vino
Cerveza

Lesson 7

Activity A   1 Buen provecho.; 2 La cuenta, por favor.; 3 ¡Está delicioso!; 4 ¿Puedo ver la carta de vinos?

Activity B   1 b; 2 a; 3 b; 4 a

Your Turn   Answers may vary.

Lesson 8

Activity A   1 quiere; 2 queremos; 3 quieren; 4 Quiere

Activity B

1 Quiero el pollo de aperitivo.; 2 No quiero queso de aperitivo.; 3 Quiero el pescado de plato principal.; 4 No quiero carne de plato principal.; 5 Quiero pastel de postre.; 6 No quiero helado de postre.

Review

Activity A

De almuerzo (querer)
1 Quiero comer sopa y beber agua.; 2 Quieres comer sopa y beber agua.; 3 Quiere comer sopa y beber agua.; 4 Queremos comer sopa y beber agua.; 5 Ustedes quieren comer sopa y beber agua.; 6 Ellos quieren comer sopa y beber agua.
De cena (preferir)
1 Prefiero comer carne y beber cerveza.; 2 Prefieres comer carne y beber cerveza.; 3 Prefiere comer carne y beber cerveza.; 4 Preferimos comer carne y beber cerveza.; 5 Prefieren comer carne y beber cerveza.; 6 Prefieren comer carne y beber cerveza.

Activity B

Café Español
Menú

Aperitivo
Plato de queso y frutas
Ensalada
Plato Principal
Pollo con vegetales
Carne con papas
Pescado
Postre
Pastel de chocolate

Activity C
Julio   Tengo hambre.
Eva   ¿Qué quieres comer?
Julio   Tengo ganas de comer pollo.
Eva   Vamos a cenar.
In the car
Julio   ¿Dónde está el restaurante?
Eva   Está ahí.
At the restaurant before eating
Eva   ¿Qué quieres de plato principal?
Julio   Quiero pollo.
At the restaurant after eating
Eva   Mesero, la cuenta, por favor.

Unit 6 Lesson 1

Activity A

1 c; 2 d; 3 b; 4 a

Activity B

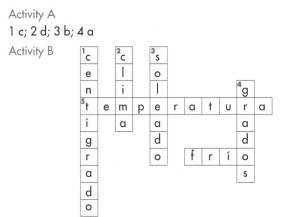

Lesson 2

Activity A

¿Cómo está el clima en Colombia?; Hace calor y está soleado.; ¿Cuál es la temperatura?; Estamos a cuarenta y tres grados centígrados.; ¿Sí? Aquí hace frío. Estamos a siete grados centígrados.

Activity B

1 a ; 2 b; 3 b; 4 b

Activity C

1 c; 2 b; 3 a; 4 d

Lesson 3

Activity A

¿Cuál es la temperatura?	¿Cómo está el clima?
35°C	Hace calor.
6°C	Hace buen tiempo.
32°F	Hace frío.

Activity B   1 b; 2 d; 3 a; 4 c

Activity C   1 a; 2 a; 3 b

Lesson 4

Activity A

1 Está; 2 Está; 3 estás; 4 estoy; 5 está; 6 están; 7 estamos; 8 están

Activity B

1 está; 2 está; 3 Está; 4 Está

Your Turn   Answers will vary. Possible answers:

Estoy (muy bien/bien/mal).
Estoy en mi casa./Estoy en (city or country where you are).
Hace (buen/mal) tiempo./Está (soleado/nublado/lloviendo).
Estoy (alegre/triste).

Lesson 5

Activity A

actividades en el verano: jugar fútbol; nadar; correr
ropa de invierno: chaqueta; bufanda; guantes; botas

Activity B   1 plays soccer; 2 winter; 3 winter; 4 Argentina, 33

Lesson 6

Activity A   Answers will vary between **es divertido** and **es aburrido**.

Activity B   1 ¿Qué está haciendo?; 2 ¿Qué hace usualmente?; 3 Durante el invierno yo usualmente (viajo).; 4 Tiene razón.

Your Turn   Answers may vary. Possible answers are:

1 Ir a la playa es divertido.; 2 Lavar la ropa es aburrido.; 3 Jugar fútbol es divertido.; 4 Hacer ejercicio es aburrido.

Lesson 7

Activity A   1 las botas; 2 los guantes; 3 el sombrero; 4 la chaqueta

Activity B   1 el otoño; 2 la primavera; 3 el invierno; 4 el verano

Activity C   1 un sombrero; 2 guantes; 3 chaqueta; 4 sandalias

Lesson 8

Activity A   1 María juega fútbol.; 2 Jugamos fútbol.; 3 Juego fútbol.; 4 Juegan fútbol.

Activity B   1 Juego vólibol.; 2 Juego golf.; 3 Juego a las cartas.; 4 Juego fútbol americano.

Activity C   1 viajando; 2 jugando; 3 haciendo; 4 nadando

Activity D   1 Yo estoy viajando.; 2 Él está jugando.; 3 Ellos están corriendo.; 4 Tú estás nadando.

Review

Activity A   1 estar; 2 ser; 3 ser; 4 estar; 5 estar

Activity B   1 Yo estoy estudiando.; 2 Yo soy mexicana.; 3 Ella es de Perú.; 4 Estamos aburridos.; 5 Está lloviendo.

Activity C

```
B  P  E  V  Z  L  Z  S  C  S  H  K  W  Y  J
X  C  L  A (C  H  A  Q  U  E  T  A) W  V  V
Q  P  Y  C  X  Q  Z  M  K  D  Y  D  P  Y  C
F  D (S  L  A (P  R  I  M  A  V  E  R  A)(E
X  D (O  B  M  N  A  B  R  Z  E  K  P  E  S
Q  Á (L  F  L  M (S  O  L  E  A  D  O) I  T
F  Q  E  A (T  E  M  P  E  R  A  T  U  R  A
P  Z  Z  Z  Q  G  A  L  Q  A  W  P  E  H  R)
Y  E  S  T  Á (C  Á  L  I  D  O) D  L  L  F
A  I (J  U  G  A  R) E  G  Q  J  T  J  K  W
B  K  V  F  Z  R  H  V  R  E  P  J  U  O  D
S  Q  W  R  J  P  K  A  P  P  J  R  N  Y  U
I  T  Y  T  A  E  Á  R) D  B  X  L  Q  X  N
```

Activity D

Está lloviendo. ¿Dónde está mi paraguas?
Aquí está.
También hace frío. ¿Dónde está mi chaqueta?
Aquí está.
Mmmm, llueve mucho. ¿Dónde están mis botas?
¡Es tarde!

Challenge

Juego fútbol cuando está lloviendo.

Unit 7 Lesson 1

Activity A

1 c; 2 b; 3 b

Activity B

1a; 2 b; 3 a

Lesson 2

Activity A

1 a; 2 a; 3 b; 4 a

Activity B

1 Estoy buscando un vestido.; 2 Necesito una camisa de talla mediana.; 3 Quiero comprar una falda.; 4 Necesito una talla pequeña.

Lesson 3

Activity A

1 la camiseta; 2 los pantalones; 3 el vestido; 4 la blusa; 5 la falda

Activity B

1 a; 2 a; 3 a; 4 a

Lesson 4

Activity A

1 se; 2 nos; 3 se; 4 te

Activity B

1 visten; 2 vistes; 3 visto; 4 vestimos; 5 visten

Your Turn

yo	me	pruebo
tú	te	pruebas
usted	se	prueba
él/ella	se	prueba
nosotros/nosotras	nos	probamos
ustedes	se	prueban
ellos/ellas	se	prueban

Lesson 5

Activity A

1 b; 2 b; 3 a; 4 b

Activity B

1 a; 2 a; 3 b; 4 a

Lesson 6

Activity A

1 ¿Acepta tarjetas de débito?; 2 ¿Cuánto cuesta la falda?; 3 ¿Acepta cheques?; 4 Voy a pagar con tarjeta de crédito; 5 ¿Cuánto cuestan los pantalones?

Activity B

1 caros; 2 muy cara; 3 barato; 4 baratos

Lesson 7

Activity A

1 cheque; 2 tarjeta de débito; 3 el recibo; 4 dinero

Activity B

Tengo 500 dólares en efectivo en mi billetera. También tengo una tarjeta de crédito. Voy a comprar mucha ropa porque no hay impuesto.

Lesson 8

Activity A

1 más que; 2 menos que; 3 más que; 4 menos que

Activity B

1 Alguien; 2 Ninguna; 3 Algunos; 4 Nadie

Review

Activity A

1 Yo me pruebo la falda.; 2 Ellas se visten en la mañana.; 3 Nosotros nos probamos los pantalones.; 4 Él se viste con el mismo color.

Challenge

yo	me	divierto
tú	te	diviertes
usted	se	divierte
él/ella	se	divierte
nosotros/nosotras	nos	divertimos
ustedes	se	divierten
ellos/ellas	se	divierten

Activity B

1 La camiseta cuesta menos que la falda. La falda cuesta más que la camiseta; 2 La blusa cuesta menos que el vestido. El vestido cuesta más que la blusa.; 3 Él abrigo cuesta más que los zapatos. Los zapatos cuestan menos que el abrigo.; 4 La falda cuesta menos que la corbata. La corbata cuesta más que la falda.

Activity C

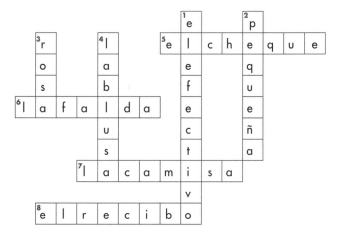

Unit 8 Lesson 1

Activity A

1 to arrive; 2 to take; 3 to walk

Activity B

1 el Mercado de San Miguel; 2 a la oficina de turismo en la Plaza Mayor; 3 Pueden tomar el autobús, el metro o pueden caminar.; 4 Quiere ver la biblioteca y las iglesias viejas.

Lesson 2

Activity A

1 la biblioteca; 2 la estación de metro; 3 la escuela; 4 la iglesia; 5 la estación de tren; 6 la parada de autobús; 7 la oficina de correos; 8 el supermercado

Activity B

1 b; 2 b; 3 a; 4 b

Lesson 3

Activity A

1 Quiero tomar el autobús. ¿Cómo llego a la parada de al autobús?; 2 Quiero tomar el tren. ¿Cómo llego a la estación de tren?; 3 Quiero tomar el metro. ¿Cómo llego a la estación de metro?

Activity B

1 ¿Dónde está la estación de tren?; 2 ¿Cómo llego a la estación de metro?; 3 La estación del tren está cerca de la escuela; 4 Vamos a conseguir un mapa.

Activity C

1 Para llegar a Plaza Mayor necesitas ir a la parada de autobús. Tienes que tomar el autobús número nueve.; 2 Para llegar a la iglesia tienes que tomar el tren.

Your Turn

Disculpe, necesito encontrar la parada de autobús. ¿Dónde está y cómo llego allí? Muchas gracias.

Lesson 4

Activity A

1 van; 2 va; 3 vamos; 4 vas

Activity B

1 ¿A dónde va Luisa?; 2 ¿A dónde va Darío?; 3 ¿A dónde va el avión?; 4 ¿A dónde van sus tíos?

Activity C

1 Ellos van al supermercado.; 2 Él va a la estación de metro; 3 Ellas van a la escuela; 4 Ella va a la iglesia.

Lesson 5

Activity A

1 b; 2 b; 3 a; 4 a

Activity B

las 10:00; las 16:00; las 17:00

Lesson 6

Activity A

1 b; 2 d; 3 e; 4 c; 5 a

Activity B

1 a; 2 a; 3 b; 4 b

Lesson 7

Activity A

1 El vuelo sale a las 12:30.; 2 ¿De qué puerta sale?; 3 ¿A qué sala llega?

Activity B

1 a; 2 b; 3 a

Activity C

1 El próximo vuelo a Puebla sale a las 17:20.; 2 Los vuelos a Madrid y Veracruz

Your Turn

El vuelo 1699, con destino a Madrid, sale a las 10:23 AM y llega a Madrid a la 1:30 PM.

Lesson 8

Activity A

1 Conoces; 2 conozco; 3 Conocemos; 4 Conocen

Activity B

1 Yo lo bebo.; 2 Ella lo estudia.; 3 Tú las conoces.; 4 Ellos los llevan.

Your Turn

Answers will vary.

Review

Activity A

Querida Clara:
Mi madre y yo estamos en Ecuador. Nosotros nos vamos a Quito mañana. ¿Tú conoces Quito? Yo lo conozco bien. Después nos vamos a Venezuela. ¿Conocen Venezuela? Un abrazo,
Paco

Activity B

Voy; mi vuelo sale a; al aeropuerto ; boleto; equipaje; pasaporte; una estación de tren; cerca de; detrás de una iglesia; quiero tomar el metro

Activity C

Augusto	¿Dónde está la oficina de correos?
Gabriela	Vamos a conseguir un mapa.
Augusto	Mira el mapa. La oficina de correos está a la derecha de la biblioteca.
Gabriela	Sí, y también está detrás del supermercado.
Augusto	Esta es la parada de autobús.
Gabriela	Sí. Ahí lo tomamos.

Challenge

yo sé; tú sabes; él/ella sabe; nosotros/nosotras sabemos; ustedes saben; ellos/ellas saben

Unit 9 Lesson 1

Activity A   1 b; 2 b; 3 b; 4 a

Activity B   1 trabajó; 2 escribió; 3 cultura; 4 empieza

Lesson 2

Activity A

salón; el profesor; estudiantes; periodista; revista; estudiante

Activity B

1 a la estudiante; b el estudiante; c el profesor
2 a la oficina; b el periodista; c la periodista

Lesson 3

Activity A

1 un profesor; 2 una periodista; 3 una periodista; 4 una profesora

Activity B

1 ¿Qué quiere ser?; 2 Quiero ser un profesor.; 3 ¿Cuál es su profesión?; 4 Soy un periodista.

Your Turn   Answers may vary. Possible answers:
Hola, me llamo Ángel y soy un periodista. ¿Cuál es su profesión? Yo soy un reportero, pero quiero ser un escritor.

Lesson 4

Activity A   1 trabajaste; 2 aprendió; 3 escribimos; 4 trabajaron

Activity B

1 Yo trabajé en la oficina.; 2 Ustedes aprendieron inglés.; 3 Él vivió en Panamá.; 4 Tú comiste pollo.; 5 Ella escribió un artículo.; 6 Mariana y yo escribimos una tarjeta postal.

Lesson 5

Activity A   1 a proofreader; 2 two years; 3 Banco Popular; 4 Periódico Metro Málaga; 5 a newspaper

Activity B   1 desired position; 2 desired salary

Lesson 6

Activity A   1 c; 2 a; 3 b; 4 b

Activity B

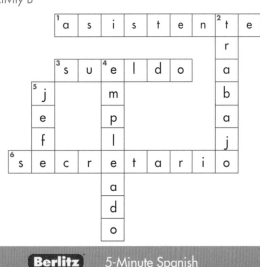

Your Turn

Answers may vary. Possible answers: Tengo 5 empleados: dos asistentes y tres secretarias. Pago 25 dólares por hora a las secretarias y 18 dólares por hora a mis asistentes.

Lesson 7

Activity A
Answers may vary.
1 más difícil; 2 más fácil; 3 más fácil; 4 más difícil

Activity B
1 ¿Por qué desea ser periodista?; 2 Me gusta ayudar; 3 ¿Cuánto tiempo ha trabajado allí?; 4 Trabajo allí desde hace dos años.

Lesson 8

Activity A
1 aprenderás; 2 trabajaré; 3 escribirán, 4 trabajaremos

Activity B
1 Estudiaré francés; 2 Ayudaré a mi familia; 3 Visitaré más a mis tíos; 4 Leeré el Quijote; 5 Corregiré mi tesis; 6 Viajaré una vez al mes

Review

Activity A

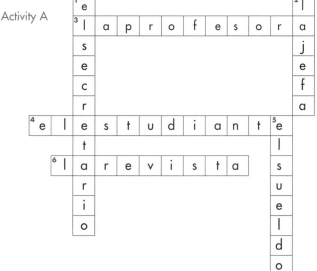

Activity B
1 ¿Cuándo trabajarán?; 2 ¿Cuándo aprendieron la canción?; 3 ¿Qué escribió ella para la revista Semana?

Activity C
Answers will vary. Possible answers:
1 Ernesto viajará a San Cristóbal la próxima semana.; 2 Veremos a Luis en la oficina.; 3 ¿Cuándo escribirá su artículo el estudiante?; 4 ¿Qué cocinarán ellos?

Activity D
1 ¿Dónde trabajarás mañana?; 2 Porque quiero ayudar a la gente.; 3 Deseo este trabajo porque es más fácil.; 4 Laura y Lola escribieron el artículo ayer.

Challenge   salario; posición

Unit 10 Lesson 1

Activity A 1 b; 2 a; 3 b; 4 b

Activity B

1 Sí, la va a ayudar.; 2 No quiere recoger la ropa.; 3 Él quiere organizar el armario.; 4 Él dice que pueden limpiar y pintar juntos.

Lesson 2

Activity A

Answers will vary. Possible answers:

Amigo	¿Vives en una casa o en un apartamento?
Yo	Vivo en un apartamento.
Amigo	¿Cuántos cuartos hay?
Yo	Hay cinco cuartos.
Amigo	¿Cuáles son los cuartos más grandes?
Yo	Los cuartos más grandes son el dormitorio y la sala.

Activity B

1 la sala; 2 la cocina; 3 el dormitorio; 4 el baño; 5 el comedor; 6 el armario

Lesson 3

Activity A

1 ¿Puedes ayudarme?; 2 No, no puedo ayudarte; 3 ¿Qué quieres que hagas?; 4 Ahora mismo.

Activity B

1 ¿Puedes ayudarme?; 2 Sí, puedo ayudarte. ¿Qué quieres que haga?; 3 Recoge la ropa.; 4 Ahora mismo.

Lesson 4

Activity A

1 puedes; 2 puede; 3 pueden; 4 puede

Activity B

Recoge la ropa.; Pinta el cuarto.; Organiza el armario.; Limpia el suelo.

Lesson 5

Activity A

1 a; 2 b; 3 a; 4 b

Activity B

1 Catalina tuvo una buena semana.; 2 Estuvo divertido.; 3 Ella fue al club.; 4 Ella fue con su novio.

Activity C

1 Fue a un concierto de Rock.; 2 Fue a comprar ropa con su madre.; 3 Fue al club con su novio.

Lesson 6

Activity A

1 Ellas fueron al bar.; 2 Ellos fueron al cine.; 3 Ellos fueron al teatro.; 4 Ellos fueron a un concierto.

Activity B

1 ayer; 2 anteayer; 3 la semana pasada; 4 anoche

Activity C

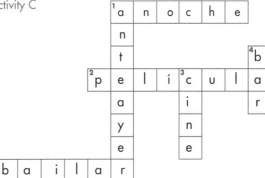

Lesson 7

Activity A 1 ¿Qué hiciste la semana pasada?; 2 ¿Qué quieres hacer?; 3 Quiero salir.; 4 Quiero quedarme en casa.

Activity B

1 **Eduardo** ¿Qué quieres hacer esta noche?

2 **Estrella** Quiero quedarme en casa esta noche.

3 **Eduardo** Pero, quiero salir de la casa. ¿Quieres bailar?

4 **Estrella** Fui a bailar con mis amigos ayer.

5 **Eduardo** ¿Vamos al cine?

6 **Estrella** Fui al cine anoche.

7 **Eduardo** Nos quedamos en casa esta noche. Eduardo decide quedarse en casa esa noche.

Your Turn Answer will vary. Possible answer: Esta noche quiero quedarme en casa y ver una película.

Lesson 8

Activity A 1 ir; 2 ser; 3 ir; 4 ser

Activity B 1 fui; 2 fuiste; 3 fue; 4 fuimos; 5 fueron; 6 fueron

Activity C 1 I went to my mother's house last night.; 2 You went to work yesterday.; 3 He was my boss for two years.; 4 We went to the game the day before yesterday.; 5 They dated during the summer.; 6 My grandparents went to Quito.

Your Turn Answers will vary. Possible answers: Anoche fui a la iglesia. Anteayer fui a bailar.

Review

Activity A 1 baño; 2 película; 3 bailar; 4 pintar; 5 cocina

Activity B 1 b; 2 a; 3 b; 4 a

Activity C Answers may vary. 1 Anoche fui al cine.; 2 La película fue de comedia.; 3 Los postres fueron helados de vainilla y chocolate; 4. No, no fuimos al concierto.

Activity D 1 Ayúdame a limpiar.; 2 Ayúdeme a pintar.; 3 Recojan la ropa.; 4 Recoge el libro.

Challenge 1 ¿Puedes ayudarme a limpiar?; 2 ¿Puede ayudarme a pintar?; 3 ¿Pueden recoger la ropa?; 4 ¿Puedes recoger ese libro?

Unit 11 Lesson 1

Activity A

1 a; 2 b; 3 b; 4 b

Activity B

1 a; 2 b; 3 a

Activity C

Hola, Melisa. Quiero jugar el lunes. ¿Puedes jugar?

Lesson 2

Activity A

1 la natación; 2 el tenis; 3 el fútbol; 4 el ciclismo

Activity B

1 el gimnasio; 2 peso; 3 gordo; 4 delgada, sana; 5 estrés;
6 enfermo

Activity C

1 b; 2 a; 3 a; 4 b

Lesson 3

Activity A

1 Estoy sano.; 2 Quiero estar en forma.; 3 ¿Cómo se siente?; 4
Quiero bajar de peso.

Activity B

1 a; 2 a; 3 b; 4 a; 5 a

Your Turn

Me siento mal. Estoy enferma. Necesito bajar de peso.

Lesson 4

Activity A

1 Él va a escribir.; 2 Voy a bailar.; 3 Ellos van a estudiar.;
4 Nosotros vamos a jugar.; 5 Tú vas a cocinar.; 6 Ella va a correr.

Activity B

2 ¿Cuándo va a llamar?; 3 ¿Cuándo van a vivir en México?;
4 ¿Quién va a llamar?; 5 ¿Quiénes van a tomar cerveza?;
6 ¿Quién va a limpiar los cuartos?

Your Turn

Va a llover.; Ellos van a cenar.; Él va a jugar béisbol.; Ella va a
escribir.

Lesson 5

Activity A   1 a; 2 a; 3 b; 4 a

Activity B   1 b; 2 b; 3 a; 4 b; 5 a

Activity C

La medicina para el resfriado ayuda con la fiebre y la tos y la
medicina para la tos ayuda con el dolor de garganta. Las dos
medicinas alivian la fiebre. La medicina de la tos alivia la fiebre
y la medicina del resfriado alivia el dolor de garganta.

Lesson 6

Activity A

1 b; 2 b; 3 b

Activity B

1. Él tiene dolor de estómago.; 2 Ella tiene tos.; 3 Él tiene dolor
de cabeza.; 4 Ella tiene dolor de muela.

Your Turn

Answers will vary. Possible answers: Él tiene tos y dolor de
garganta. Necesita medicina para el resfriado y medicina para
la tos.

Lesson 7

Activity A

1 Me duele la mano.; 2 Le duele la espalda.; 3 Me duelen las
piernas.; 4 Le duele el brazo.

Activity B

Answers may vary. Possible answers: Estoy enfermo. Tengo
fiebre. Me duele la cabeza y la espalda.

Activity C

Answers may vary. Possible answers: Carlos Ríos tiene fiebre.
Le duele la cabeza y la espalda. Necesita medicina para el
resfriado. El doctor le va a dar una receta.

Lesson 8

Activity A

Answers may vary.

Activity B

1 A veces juego tenis.; 2 Siempre voy al gimnasio.;
3 Usualmente estoy sano.; 4 Juego tenis una vez a la semana.;
5 Nunca tomo medicina.; 6 Corro todos los días.

Activity C

1 ¿Siempre vas a Cartagena en julio?; 2 ¿Usualmente viajas en
el verano?; 3 ¿Almuerza Esteban en la casa todos los días?

Your Turn

1 Voy al cine cada mes.; 2 Hago ejercicios a veces; 3 Nunca voy
al gimnasio; 4 Siempre voy al trabajo.

Review

Activity A

Me siento bien.; Estoy sana.; No voy a ver a la dentista.; Tengo
dolor de estómago.; No quiero ir al doctor.; Hago ejercicio
porque quiero bajar de peso.

Activity B

1 Me duele la cabeza.; 2 Voy a vivir en Perú.; 3 Hago ejercicio
dos veces a la semana.; 4 Teresa va a correr en el parque.; 5
Vas a cocinar la cena.; 6 Me duelen los pies.

Activity C

1 ciclismo; 2 tenis; 3 enfermo ; 4 medicina; 5 fiebre; 6 dentista

Challenge

Answers may vary. Possible answers:
Mañana voy a cocinar arroz con pollo.
A menudo veo películas para divertirme.
El próximo mes voy a viajar.

Photo Credits

Interior

p. 8: (TR) © Jason Stitt 2008/Shutterstock, Inc., (RC) © Jason Stitt 2008/Shutterstock, Inc., (BR) © Edyta Pawlowska 2008/Shutterstock, Inc., (TL) © Orange Line Media 2008/Shutterstock, Inc.; p. 9: (TR) © Yuri Arcurs 2008/Shutterstock, Inc., (TRC) © Dmitriy Shironosov 2008/Shutterstock, Inc., (BRC) © 2008 Jupiter Images, Inc., (BR) © 2008 Jupiter Images, Inc.; p. 10: (TL) © Raia 2008/Shutterstock, Inc., (B, Bkgrd) © Lars Christensen 2008/Shutterstock, Inc., (BL, Inset) © Awe Inspiring Images 2008/Shutterstock, Inc., (BLC, Inset) © Matt Trommer 2008/Shutterstock, Inc., (BRC, Inset) © Movit 2008/Shutterstock, Inc., (BR, Inset) © 2008 Jupiter Images, Inc., (TR) © ZTS 2008/Shutterstock, Inc.; p. 11: (TL) © Lisa F. Young 2008/Shutterstock, Inc., (TR) © 2008 Jupiter Images, Inc., (TRC) © 2008 Jupiter Images, Inc., (CL) © Bobby Deal 2008/Shutterstock, Inc., (CR) © 2008 Jupiter Images, Inc., (CLC) © 2008 Jupiter Images, Inc., (CRC) © Yuri Arcurs 2008/Shutterstock, Inc., (BLL) © 2008 Jupiter Images, Inc., (BL) © Yuri Arcurs 2008/Shutterstock, Inc., (BLC) © Konstantynov 2008/Shutterstock, Inc., (BR) © Andresr 2008/Shutterstock, Inc.; p. 13: (TL) © Sandra G 2008/Shutterstock, Inc., (TR) © Pilar Echevarria 2008/Shutterstock, Inc., (TRC) © Lukas Wroblewski 2008/Shutterstock, Inc., (CRT) © Aura Castro 2008/Shutterstock, Inc., (CRB) © Edyta Pawlowska 2008/Shutterstock, Inc., (BLT) © photobank.ch 2008/Shutterstock, Inc., (BLC) © Supri Suharjoto 2008/Shutterstock, Inc., (BL) © 2008 Jupiter Images, Inc., (BLB) © Niels Quist 2008/Shutterstock, Inc., (BRC) © Daniel Wiedemann 2008/Shutterstock, Inc.; p. 14: (C) © Raphael Ramirez Lee 2008/Shutterstock, Inc., (B) © Silvia Bukovac 2008/Shutterstock, Inc.; p. 15: (T) © Yuri Arcurs 2008/Shutterstock, Inc., (B) © Dmitriy Shironosov 2008/Shutterstock, Inc.; p. 16: © Galyna Andrushko 2008/Shutterstock, Inc.; p. 17: (TL, Inset) © Pavel Sazonov 2008/Shutterstock, Inc., (TLC, Inset) © Nick Stubbs 2008/Shutterstock, Inc., (TRC, Inset) © Dario Diament 2008/Shutterstock, Inc., (TR, Inset) © Khoroshunova Olga 2008/Shutterstock, Inc., (BLL, Inset) © Daniel Gale 2008/Shutterstock, Inc., (BL, Inset) © Juris Korjakins 2008/Shutterstock, Inc., (BLC, Inset) © Stepan Jezek 2008/Shutterstock, Inc., (BRC, Inset) © Eduardo Cervantes 2008/Shutterstock, Inc., (BR, Inset) © Elena Elisseeva 2008/Shutterstock, Inc., (C) © Doug Raphael 2008/Shutterstock, Inc., (BR) © Kiselev Andrey Valerevich 2008/Shutterstock, Inc.; p. 18: (TLL) © photobank.ch 2008/Shutterstock, Inc., (TLC) © Yuri Arcurs 2008/Shutterstock, Inc., (TLR) © vgstudio 2008/Shutterstock, Inc., (TR, Bkgrd) © iofoto 2008/Shutterstock, Inc., (TR, Inset) © Stacy Barnett 2008/Shutterstock, Inc., (CLL) © BESTWEB 2008/Shutterstock, Inc., (CLC) © Lexx 2008/Shutterstock, Inc., (CLR) © Alexey Nikolaew 2008/Shutterstock, Inc., (B) © Vibrant Image Studio 2008/Shutterstock, Inc., (BLL) © Vladimir Melnik 2008/Shutterstock, Inc., (BLC) © Denise Kappa 2008/Shutterstock, Inc., (BLR) © MalibuBooks 2008/Shutterstock, Inc., (BCL) © fckncg 2008/Shutterstock, Inc., (BCR) © Hannu Lilvaar 2008/Shutterstock, Inc., (R, Bkgrd) © Arthur Eugene Preston 2008/Shutterstock, Inc., (LL, Inset) © Kristian Sekulic 2008/Shutterstock, Inc., (LC, Inset) © Sandy Maya Matzen 2008/Shutterstock, Inc., (C, Inset) © Galina Barskaya 2008/Shutterstock, Inc., (RC, Inset) © Rob Wilson 2008/Shutterstock, Inc., (RR, Inset) © Luminis 2008/Shutterstock, Inc.; p. 19: (T) © Nagy-Bagoly Arpad 2008/Shutterstock, Inc., (L) © Yuri Arcurs 2008/Shutterstock, Inc., (CL) © Dmitriy Shironosov 2008/Shutterstock, Inc., (CRL) © Erik Lam 2008/Shutterstock, Inc., (CRC) © Suponev Vladimir Mihajlovich 2008/Shutterstock, Inc., (CRR) © mlorenz 2008/Shutterstock, Inc., (B) © Vaclav Volrab 2008/Shutterstock, Inc., (BR) © Doug Raphael 2008/Shutterstock, Inc.; p. 20: (TL) © Andresr 2008/Shutterstock, Inc., (TR) © Ustyujanin 2008/Shutterstock, Inc., (CL) © Andrey Armyagov 2008/Shutterstock, Inc., (CRL) © Margo Harrison 2008/Shutterstock, Inc., CR) © Yuri Arcurs 2008/Shutterstock, Inc., (CRR) © Hannu Lilvaar 2008/Shutterstock, Inc., (CRB) © melkerw 2008/Shutterstock, Inc., (BL) © pandapaw 2008/Shutterstock, Inc., (BLC) © Rafa Irusta 2008/Shutterstock, Inc., ((BR) © Kiselev Andrey Valerevich 2008/Shutterstock, Inc.; p. 21: © Sam DCruz 2008/Shutterstock, Inc.; p. 22: (TL) © Scott Waldron 2008/Shutterstock, Inc., (BR) © Jason Stitt 2008/Shutterstock, Inc.; p. 23: (TL) © 2008 Jupiter Images, Inc., (TR) © J2008 upiter Images, Inc., (TRC) © J2008 upiter Images, Inc., (C) © David Gilder 2008/Shutterstock, Inc., (BL) © Andy Lim 2008/Shutterstock, Inc., (BRC) © J2008 upiter Images, Inc., (BR) © J2008 upiter Images, Inc.; p. 24: (TL) © 2008 Jupiter Images, Inc., (TR) © Monkey Business Images 2008/Shutterstock, Inc., (RC) © Andrejs Pidjass 2008/Shutterstock, Inc., (BR) © Donna Heatfield 2008/Shutterstock, Inc.; p. 25: (TL) © Nick Stubbs 2008/Shutterstock, Inc., (TLC) © Daniela Mangiuca 2008/Shutterstock, Inc., (TR) © Vladimir Mucibabic 2008/Shutterstock, Inc., (LCL) © Tomasz Pietryszek 2008/Shutterstock, Inc., (LCR) © Michael Ransburg 2008/Shutterstock, Inc., (LC) © Philip Date 2008/Shutterstock, Inc., (BL) © Raia 2008/Shutterstock, Inc.; p. 26: (T, Bkgrd) © yurok 2008/Shutterstock, Inc., (T, Inset) © 2008 Jupiter Images, Inc., (L, Inset) © Stephen Mcsweeny 2008/Shutterstock, Inc., (R) © Steve Luker 2008/Shutterstock, Inc., (R, Inset) © Tatiana Strelkova 2008/Shutterstock, Inc., (C, Inset) © Michelle Marsan 2008/Shutterstock, Inc., (CR) © MaxFX 2008/Shutterstock, Inc., (BC) © MaxFX 2008/Shutterstock, Inc., (BRC) © Steve Luker 2008/Shutterstock, Inc., (BR) © Bart Everett 2008/Shutterstock, Inc.; p. 27: (TL) © Andresr 2008/Shutterstock, Inc., (TR) © laurent hamels 2008/Shutterstock, Inc., (BR) © Fatini Zulnaidi 2008/Shutterstock, Inc.; p. 28: (TL) © Konstantin Remizov 2008/Shutterstock, Inc., (BL) © Leo Blanchette 2008/Shutterstock, Inc.; p. 29: (TR) © Lukyanov Mikhail 2008/Shutterstock, Inc., (TRC) © Mandy Godbehear 2008/Shutterstock, Inc., (LC) © Karen Struthers 2008/Shutterstock, Inc., (RC) © Monkey Business Images 2008/Shutterstock, Inc., (BRC) © Monkey Business Images 2008/Shutterstock, Inc., (BR) © Monkey Business Images 2008/Shutterstock, Inc.; p. 30: (T) © Rafa Irusta 2008/Shutterstock, Inc., (TL) © Gina Sanders 2008/Shutterstock, Inc., (TLC) © 2008 Jupiter Images, Inc., (TRC) © iofoto 2008/Shutterstock, Inc., (TR) © Morgan Lane Photography 2008/Shutterstock, Inc., (CL) © tinatka 2008/Shutterstock, Inc., (CR) © Elena Ray 2008/Shutterstock, Inc., (BL) © George Dolgikh 2008/Shutterstock, Inc., (BC) © David Hyde 2008/Shutterstock, Inc., (BRC) © J. Helgason 2008/Shutterstock, Inc., (BR) © Julian Rovagnati 2008/Shutterstock, Inc.; p. 32: (TR) © Gelpi 2008/Shutterstock, Inc., (RC) © 2008 Jupiter Images, Inc., (B) © Phil Date 2008/Shutterstock, Inc.; p. 33: (T) © Dmitriy Shironosov 2008/Shutterstock, Inc., (TRC) © Simone van den Berg 2008/Shutterstock, Inc., (TR) © 2008 Jupiter Images, Inc., (BL) © icyimage 2008/Shutterstock, Inc., (BLC) © Tomasz Trojanowski 2008/Shutterstock, Inc., (BRL) © Dmitry Yashkin 2008/Shutterstock, Inc., (BRB) © Kurhan 2008/Shutterstock, Inc., (BRC) © Ustyujanin 2008/Shutterstock, Inc., (BR) © RTimages 2008/Shutterstock, Inc.; p. 34: (BL) © Mike Flippo 2008/Shutterstock, Inc., (BR) © Pakhnyushcha 2008/Shutterstock, Inc.; p. 35: (T) © Christian Wheatley 2008/Shutterstock, Inc., (TL) © Simon Krzic 2008/Shutterstock, Inc., (TLC) © Edyta Pawlowska 2008/Shutterstock, Inc., (TC) © MWProductions 2008/Shutterstock, Inc., (TRC) © Dusaleev Viatcheslav 2008/Shutterstock, Inc., (TR) © Olga Lyubkina 2008/Shutterstock, Inc.; p. 36: (CL) © Andresr 2008/Shutterstock, Inc., (CR) © T-Design 2008/Shutterstock, Inc., (B) © Ivan Jelisavic 2008/Shutterstock, Inc., (BL) © Jason Stitt 2008/Shutterstock, Inc., (BR) © Dimitrije Paunovic 2008/Shutterstock, Inc., (Bkgrd) © khz 2008/Shutterstock, Inc.; p. 37: (TL) © Vibrant Image Studio 2008/Shutterstock, Inc., (TR) © Ersler Dmitry 2008/Shutterstock, Inc., (TRC) © Jeanne Hatch 2008/Shutterstock, Inc., (L) © iofoto 2008/Shutterstock, Inc., (CL) © iofoto 2008/Shutterstock, Inc., (BL) © iofoto 2008/Shutterstock, Inc., (BRC) © Jaren Jai Wicklund 2008/Shutterstock, Inc., (BR) © Adam Borkowski 2008/Shutterstock, Inc.; p. 38: (TL) © Lisa F. Young 2008/Shutterstock, Inc., (TRC) © Martin Valigursky 2008/Shutterstock, Inc., (TR) © Monkey Business Images 2008/Shutterstock, Inc., (RCT) © Vibrant Image Studio 2008/Shutterstock, Inc., (RCB) © Monkey Business Images 2008/Shutterstock, Inc., (R) © Sonya Etchison 2008/Shutterstock, Inc., (BRC) © Denise Kappa 2008/Shutterstock, Inc., (BR) © Monkey Business Images 2008/Shutterstock, Inc.; p. 39: (TL) © Evgeny V. Kan 2008/Shutterstock, Inc., (TR) © Carme Balcells 2008/Shutterstock, Inc., (L) © Sandra G 2008/Shutterstock, Inc., (LC) © Kurhan 2008/Shutterstock, Inc., (RC) © Simon Krzic 2008/Shutterstock, Inc., (C) © Konstantin Sutyagin 2008/Shutterstock, Inc., (R) © Carme Balcells 2008/Shutterstock, Inc., (BL) © Lexx 2008/Shutterstock, Inc., (BLC) © Allgord 2008/Shutterstock, Inc., (BRC) © Sandra G 2008/Shutterstock, Inc., (BR) © Andriy Goncharenko 2008/Shutterstock, Inc., (BBL) © Dagmara Ponikiewska 2008/Shutterstock, Inc., (BBR) © KSR 2008/Shutterstock, Inc.; p. 40: (TL) © Lisa F. Young 2008/Shutterstock, Inc., (B) © Elena Ray 2008/Shutterstock, Inc., (BL) © Najin 2008/Shutterstock, Inc., (BR) © Elena Ray 2008/Shutterstock, Inc.; p. 41: (TL) © Losevsky Pavel 2008/Shutterstock, Inc., (TR) © Ustyujanin 2008/Shutterstock, Inc., (B) © Elena Ray 2008/Shutterstock, Inc., (BL) © Elena Ray 2008/Shutterstock, Inc., (BLC) © Vitezslav Halamka 2008/Shutterstock, Inc., (BRC) © Vitezslav Halamka 2008/Shutterstock, Inc., (BR) © Robin Mackenzie 2008/Shutterstock, Inc.; p. 42: (TL) © Serghei Starus 2008/Shutterstock, Inc., (TLC) © Jaimie Duplass 2008/Shutterstock, Inc., (BL) © Rui Vale de Sousa 2008/Shutterstock, Inc., (BLC) © Steve Snowden 2008/Shutterstock, Inc., (BR) © 2008 Jupiter Images, Inc.; p. 43: (TL) © Monkey Business Images 2008/Shutterstock, Inc., (TR) © Sandra G 2008/Shutterstock, Inc., (BL) © Monkey Business Images 2008/Shutterstock, Inc., (BR) © Konstantin Sutyagin 2008/Shutterstock, Inc.; p. 44: (TL) © Sergey Rusakov 2008/Shutterstock, Inc., (TLC) © Joe Gough 2008/Shutterstock, Inc., (TR) © RexRover 2008/Shutterstock, Inc., (TRC) © Valentyn Volkov 2008/Shutterstock, Inc., (CR) © Rudchenko Liliia 2008/Shutterstock, Inc., (R) © imageZebra 2008/Shutterstock, Inc., (BL) © Ljupco Smokovski 2008/Shutterstock, Inc., (BLC) © Peter Polak 2008/Shutterstock, Inc., (BRC) © Edyta Pawlowska 2008/Shutterstock, Inc., (BR) © Edyta Pawlowska 2008/Shutterstock, Inc.; p. 45: (TL) © Edyta Pawlowska 2008/Shutterstock, Inc., (TRC) © Dusan Zidar 2008/Shutterstock, Inc., (TR) © Supri Suharjoto 2008/Shutterstock, Inc., (R) © Edw 2008/Shutterstock, Inc., (RC) © Monkey Business Images 2008/Shutterstock, Inc., (BLC) © JanP 2008/Shutterstock, Inc., (BL) © Viktor1 2008/Shutterstock, Inc., (BR) © 2008 Jupiter Images, Inc.; p. 46: (TL) © Ana Blazic 2008/Shutterstock, Inc., (TR) © Alexander Shalamov 2008/Shutterstock, Inc., (R) © Phil Date 2008/Shutterstock, Inc., (BR) © Dragan Trifunovic 2008/Shutterstock, Inc.; p. 47: (TL) © Steve Luker 2008/Shutterstock, Inc., (BL) © Andre Nantel 2008/Shutterstock, Inc.; p. 48: (TL) © 2008 Jupiter Images, Inc., (TLC) © Viktor1 2008/Shutterstock, Inc., (TRC) © Robyn Mackenzie 2008/Shutterstock, Inc., (TR) © Joe Gough 2008/Shutterstock, Inc., (L) © Jackie Carvey 2008/Shutterstock, Inc., (LC) © Anna Nizami 2008/Shutterstock, Inc.; (B) © Andrejs Pidjass 2008/Shutterstock, Inc., (BL) © Sarune Zurbaite 2008/Shutterstock, Inc., (BLC) © Bochkarev Photography 2008/Shutterstock, Inc., (BRC) © Liv Friis-Larsen 2008/Shutterstock, Inc., (BR) © Kheng Guan Toh 2008/Shutterstock, Inc., p. 49: (TL) © Rene Jansa 2008/Shutterstock, Inc., (TRC) © Joe Gough 2008/Shutterstock, Inc., (TR) © Valentin Mosichev 2008/Shutterstock, Inc., (CR) © Olga Lyubkina 2008/Shutterstock, Inc., (R) © Joe Gough 2008/Shutterstock, Inc., (BL) © 2008 Jupiter Images, Inc., (BRC) © Paul Maguire 2008/Shutterstock, Inc., (BR) © Viktor1 2008/Shutterstock, Inc.; p. 50: (TL) © 2008 Jupiter Images, Inc., (BL) © Alfred Wekelo 2008/Shutterstock, Inc., (BR) © Keith Wheatley 2008/Shutterstock, Inc.; p. 51: (TL) © Lisa F. Young 2008/Shutterstock, Inc., (BL) © David P. Smith 2008/Shutterstock, Inc., (BLC) © Dusan Zidar 2008/Shutterstock, Inc., (BRC) © David P. Smith 2008/